George Payn Quackenbos

Primary History of the United States

Made Easy and Interesting for Beginners

George Payn Quackenbos

Primary History of the United States
Made Easy and Interesting for Beginners

ISBN/EAN: 9783743399235

Manufactured in Europe, USA, Canada, Australia, Japa

Cover: Foto ©ninafisch / pixelio.de

Manufactured and distributed by brebook publishing software (www.brebook.com)

George Payn Quackenbos

Primary History of the United States

PRIMARY
HISTORY OF THE UNITED STATES:

MADE EASY AND INTERESTING FOR BEGINNERS.

BY

G. P. QUACKENBOS, A.M.,

PRINCIPAL OF "THE COLLEGIATE SCHOOL," N. Y.; AUTHOR OF "ILLUSTRATED SCHOOL HISTORY OF THE U. S.," "A NATURAL PHILOSOPHY," "FIRST LESSONS IN COMPOSITION," "ADVANCED COURSE OF COMPOSITION AND RHETORIC," ETC.

NEW YORK:
D. APPLETON & COMPANY, 443 & 445 BROADWAY.
1867.

PREFACE.

FIRST books, on any subject, should be simple and attractive. The beginner should never be discouraged by words that he does not understand, or sentences of great length and complicated structure. He should find his text-book interesting, and be won to study by the pleasant trains of thought it suggests and charms of style and story. He will otherwise be apt to conceive a dislike to the subject treated, and may feel the ill effects of a bad beginning throughout his whole subsequent course of study.

These principles have been kept in view during the preparation of the present volume. The author has here endeavored to present the history of our country so clearly that it may be studied with profit at a very early age. In the belief that simplicity is quite different from puerility, a clear style, a natural arrangement, and short sentences have been aimed at, rather than childish expressions. Leading events are presented, but without any repulsive array of minute details, dates, or figures.

We all know the fondness of the young for stories; truthful anecdotes have therefore been interspersed throughout. To please the eye, as well as awaken thought, numerous engravings, designed with strict regard to historic truth, have been introduced. The form of a continuous narrative has been adopted as preferable for reading purposes, but questions bringing out the leading facts are presented at the end of each lesson, which may be used by the learner in preparing himself and by the teacher at recitation.

It is hoped that this book will be found comprehensive and thorough, as well as easy and interesting. The wants of Primary Schools have been particularly consulted in its preparation. Used independently, it is believed that it will give a fair and correct idea of our country's history; when a more extended course is desired, it may with advantage be followed by the author's "Illustrated School History of the United States".

NEW YORK, *August* 1, 1860

ENTERED, according to Act of Congress, in the year 1860,
BY G. P. QUACKENBOS,
In the Clerk's Office of the District Court of the United States for the Southern District of New York.

CONTENTS.

LESSON		PAGE
I.	Four Hundred Years ago,	5
II.	Christopher Columbus,	7
III.	The Discovery of America,	11
IV.	Later Voyages of Columbus.—Cabot,	14
V.	Balboa.—Magellan.—Cortez,	17
VI.	French Discoveries.—De Soto,	20
VII.	The American Indians,	24
VIII.	The First Settlements,	28
IX.	Captain John Smith,	31
X.	The Virginia Colony,	35
XI.	Dutch Settlements.—Henry Hudson,	38
XII.	The Pilgrim Fathers,	41
XIII.	The Plymouth Colony,	44
XIV.	Other New England Colonies,	47
XV.	Connecticut.—The Pequod War,	50
XVI.	Maryland.—Delaware.—New Jersey,	53
XVII.	King Philip's War,	56
XVIII.	Virginia.—Indian Troubles.—Bacon's Rebellion,	60
XIX.	Carolina.—Pennsylvania,	63
XX.	Indian Missions.—French Explorers,	67
XXI.	King William's War,	70
XXII.	Queen Anne's War.—The South-west.—Georgia founded,	72
XXIII.	Washington's Expedition,	75
XXIV.	French and Indian War.—Braddock's Defeat,	78
XXV.	Close of the French and Indian War,	81
XXVI.	Troubles with the Governors,	85
XXVII.	Causes of the Revolution,	87
XXVIII.	Commencement of the Revolution,	91

CONTENTS.

LESSON		PAGE
XXIX.	Capture of Ticonderoga.—Ethan Allen,	95
XXX.	Battle of Bunker Hill,	98
XXXI.	Invasion of Canada.—Siege of Boston,	101
XXXII.	Attack on Charleston.—Declaration of Independence,	104
XXXIII.	Battle of Long Island,	108
XXXIV.	Washington's Retreat.—Trenton.—Princeton,	111
XXXV.	Burgoyne's Campaign,	115
XXXVI.	Brandywine.—Germantown.—Valley Forge,	119
XXXVII.	Monmouth.—Wyoming.—Movements in the South,	122
XXXVIII.	Paul Jones.—Francis Marion,	125
XXXIX.	Hanging Rock.—Camden.—Arnold's Treason,	129
XL.	King's Mountain.—Cowpens.—Guilford Court House,	133
XLI.	Eutaw.—Yorktown.—Close of the Revolution,	136
XLII.	Formation of a Constitution,	140
XLIII.	Washington's Two Terms,	143
XLIV.	John Adams.—Thomas Jefferson,	147
XLV.	Jefferson's Second Term.—James Madison,	151
XLVI.	Battle of Tippecanoe.—War with England,	154
XLVII.	Reverses on Land: Triumphs on the Ocean,	157
XLVIII.	The War in the North-west,	160
XLIX.	Pike's Expedition.—Fort Stephenson.—Lake Erie;	163
L.	Harrison's Invasion of Canada.—Creek War,	166
LI.	Close of the War of 1812,	171
LII.	James Monroe.—John Quincy Adams,	175
LIII.	Andrew Jackson,	178
LIV.	Martin Van Buren.—Harrison and Tyler,	181
LV.	James K. Polk.—Mexican War,	183
LVI.	Taylor and Fillmore,	187
LVII.	Franklin Pierce.—James Buchanan,	189

PRIMARY HISTORY OF THE UNITED STATES.

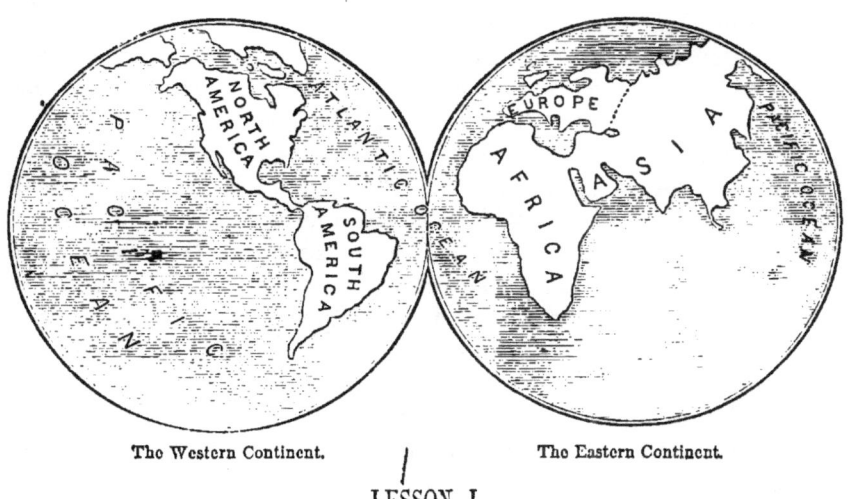

The Western Continent. | The Eastern Continent.

LESSON I.

FOUR HUNDRED YEARS AGO.

1. The Earth is round, like a ball. It contains two large divisions of land, called Continents. One lies in the east, and is called the Eastern Continent. The other lies in the west, and is called the Western Continent. These two continents are separated on one side by the broad Atlantic Ocean, and on the other by the Pacific, which is still broader. The map given above shows these continents and oceans.

2. The United States, in which we live, is part of North America, and lies in the Western Continent. Europe, Asia, and Africa, form the Eastern Continent. Those who want to go from one con-

tinent to the other, have to sail many miles, across either the Atlantic or the Pacific.

3. Now, our gallant sailors think nothing of making such a voyage. But there was a time when even the bravest were afraid to venture far out upon the Ocean. Their vessels were not so large or so well shaped as ours; and they feared, if they went too far away from land, they would never find the way back.

4. Four hundred years ago, men did not know so much about the Earth as they do now. They thought that it was flat, instead of round. They knew nothing of the Western Continent. They were afraid of the broad ocean. They supposed that those who kept sailing west would either reach the end of the Earth and fall off, or meet with dreadful gales and whirlpools. Some thought that the unknown waters to the west were filled with frightful monsters, and that it was wicked to try to sail there. So they left the Atlantic mostly unexplored. The farthest land that was known towards the west was the islands called the A-zores', about 800 miles west of Portugal.

5. Four hundred years ago, the land we inhabit looked very different from what it now does. There were no great cities in it then; no large farms, with fields of waving grain; no comfortable houses, with smoke curling up from their chimney-tops; no horses or cattle in the meadows; no fences, no bridges, no roads; no steamboats or sailing-vessels on the rivers; no white men, to give life to the whole.

6. In place of these, there were giant trees, thick woods, and rolling prairies. Deer, bears, and wolves abounded. There were fair streams, but no signs of life on them except the busy beaver. Here and there was a rude hut, covered with bark or skins; and dark, half-naked figures stole through the tangled brush-wood.

7. And what has so changed the appearance of the country?— Its discovery by Europeans. They found it a fruitful and pleasant land. They came over to it in great numbers. They cut down the woods, laid out farms, tilled the soil, and built villages and cities. They made the wilderness blossom like the rose.

8. But the Western Continent might have remained unknown to Europeans till this day, had it not been for the genius of one man. That great man, the discoverer of America, was Christopher Columbus.

QUESTIONS.—1. What is the shape of the Earth? What does it contain? What are the two continents called? How are they separated? Point to them on the Map.—2. Where does the United States lie? What countries form the Eastern Continent? How can a person go from one continent to the other?—3. In old times, what did people think of a voyage across the ocean?—4. What did people think about the shape of the Earth, four hundred years ago? What did they think would happen to those who kept sailing west? What was the farthest land known towards the west?—5. What are found in this country now, that were not here four hundred years ago?—6. Describe this country, as it then looked.—7. What has so changed the appearance of our country? What have European settlers done?—8. To whom is the world indebted for the discovery of America?

LESSON II.

CHRISTOPHER COLUMBUS.

1. Columbus was born at Gen'-o-a, in Italy, a country of Europe. His parents were poor, but had him well taught. At an early age he went to sea, and visited various countries. On one occasion, the ship on which he served took fire, and he had to throw himself into the sea and swim for his life.

2. After making many voyages, Columbus became convinced that the Earth was round, and that by sailing west he would finally

reach land. If you mark an orange, and place your finger on the opposite side of it, you will reach the mark whichever way you carry your finger round. So Columbus thought that by sailing west he would arrive at Asia, just as certainly as he would by going east. He knew nothing of the Western Continent; but he supposed that Asia extended much farther east than it does, and he determined to try to reach it by launching out on the unexplored ocean.

3. The Azores, as we have said, were the most westerly land known at that day. Now, after a violent west wind, trees torn up by the roots were sometimes washed on these islands. The bodies of two men, very different in appearance from the people of Europe and Africa, had also been thrown there. These facts confirmed Columbus in his belief, and made him still more anxious to set out on a voyage of discovery.

4. But where was he to get the means? He was poor, and had no ships of his own. He could only lay his plans before the different powers of Europe, and beg their aid. First he tried his countrymen, the Genoese, but without success. Then he went to Portugal. The King of this country listened to his arguments; but, wishing to have the honor of the discovery all to himself, he basely deceived Columbus, and sent out a vessel on the proposed course under another commander. The expedition, however, failed, as it deserved to do.

5. Columbus next turned to Spain, which was then ruled by the famous Ferdinand and his wife Isabella. He had by this time become so poor that on his way to the court he had to beg for bread for himself and his little son. On his arrival, he found the King and Queen engaged in a great war with the Moors. They had no time to listen to a poor sailor whom every one laughed at. Still

Columbus would not give up. Full of his great idea, he waited for a more favorable time, supporting himself by making maps and charts.

6. At last he obtained the ear of Ferdinand, and pleaded his cause so earnestly that he almost convinced the King. But the long war had exhausted the royal treasury, and money was too scarce to be risked on an uncertainty. So Ferdinand resolved to take the advice of the wise men of his kingdom. Columbus appeared before them at Salamanca, to unfold his cherished plan. Here you see him arguing before the council.

7. But the wise men of Spain could not believe that a poor

sailor knew more than they did. How, they asked, could the Earth be round? If it were, then on the opposite side the rain would fall upward; trees would grow with their branches down; and every thing would be topsy-turvy. Objects on its surface would certainly fall off the opposite side; and, if a ship by sailing west got around there, it would never be able to climb up the side of the Earth and get back again. How could a ship sail up hill?

8. Such was the reasoning of the wise men. By their advice, the King refused to furnish Columbus the ships he wanted. Who can describe his disappointment, after waiting so many years? There was yet one chance. Perhaps Queen Isabella would listen to him with more favor. He obtained an interview with her. Alas! she too was persuaded to refuse him.

9. Almost in despair, Columbus was on the point of quitting Spain forever, when a message from Isabella recalled him to court, with the glad tidings that the Queen had changed her mind. She had determined to fit out three vessels for the enterprise, even if she had to pledge her jewels to raise the necessary money.

QUESTIONS.—1. Where was Columbus born? What is said of his parents? What did he do at an early age? What accident befell him?—2. After making many voyages, of what did Columbus become convinced? What did he suppose with respect to Asia? —3. What confirmed Columbus in his belief that the Earth was round? What was he anxious to do?—4. Why did not Columbus set out at once on his voyage? To whom did he first apply for ships? Where did he then go? What did the King of Portugal do?—5. Where did Columbus next go? By whom was Spain then ruled? What was the condition of Columbus at this time? In what did he find the King and Queen engaged? What was the consequence?—6. At last, with whom did he obtain an interview? What was the result?—7. What was the opinion of the wise men of Spain? Mention some of their arguments.—8. What conclusion did the King come to? What chance yet remained? What answer did Queen Isabella first make?—9. What happened just as Columbus was about leaving Spain? How many vessels did the Queen promise him?

LESSON III.

THE DISCOVERY OF AMERICA.

1. Here is a picture of a ship in the time of Columbus. It looks quite different from a ship of the present day. The hull is much higher out of the water than that of modern ships, and not so sharp in front. The rigging, too, is different. You see a little round box near the top of the central mast. Here a sailor was stationed to keep a look-out; and in battle men were placed there to shoot those who appeared on the enemy's deck.

2. With three such ships, two of which had no decks, Columbus set out on his voyage of discovery. So dangerous was it considered, that he could hardly get sailors enough to man his vessels. At last ninety men were obtained, and with these he sailed from Palos [*pah'-los*], a Spanish port, on the 3d of August, 1492. Columbus was now fifty-seven years old.

3. After stopping at the Canary Islands, to repair one of their vessels, Columbus and his men stood out boldly to the west on the

great ocean. Day after day they kept on their course, with nothing in sight but the sky and the sea. The sailors looked out anxiously for land; but, as none appeared, they became terribly frightened, and wanted to turn back. This Columbus would not do. He set before them the glory they would gain if they succeeded, and the anger of Queen Isabella if they should return contrary to his wishes. But, as time wore on, they became more and more alarmed. They feared they would never find the way home. They even talked of throwing Columbus overboard, and taking the ship back to Spain themselves.

4. At last Columbus had to promise that if land was not discovered within three days he would return. How anxiously he watched during that time, and how high his heart beat with hope when signs of land actually appeared! The water grew shallower. Flocks of little birds came round the vessels. A branch bearing fresh berries was found floating on the sea. A close watch was kept. Two hours after midnight, on the 12th of October, a joyful cry of *Land! Land!* was heard from one of the vessels. It was echoed on the others. The sailors were now frantic with delight. They were ready to worship Columbus, whom a little while before they had talked of throwing into the sea.

5. When day dawned, the land was plainly seen. A pleasant land it was. There were gay flowers, and tall trees with leaves and fruit such as they had never seen before. On the shore were unclad copper-colored men, gazing in wonder at the Spanish ships. They took the ships for great birds, the white sails for their wings, and the Spaniards for superior beings brought down from Heaven on their backs.

6. Columbus and his men hastened to land. Kneeling, they kissed the earth, and returned thanks for their successful voyage.

Then Columbus took possession of the country in the name of the King and Queen of Spain.

7. The land thus discovered was one of the Ba-ha'-ma Islands, in the Atlantic Ocean, between North and South America. He named it San Sal'-va-dor. Thinking that he was now in the East Indies, he called the natives INDIANS. All the islands of this region are still known as the West Indies.

8. Columbus soon left San Salvador, to make further discoveries, in the course of which he touched at Cu'-ba and Haiti [*i'-te*]. At the latter island he lost one of his ships, and left some of his men as a colony. After collecting specimens of the productions, and inducing several of the natives to embark with him, he set out to retrace his course to Spain.

9. On the return voyage, a terrific storm arose. Fearing shipwreck, Columbus wrote an account of his discoveries, and sealed it up in a cask, which he threw into the sea, hoping that if he and his men were lost it would be picked up and made known to the world. But it was not God's will that he should perish thus. His ships, though shattered, brought him safe to port. He landed amid the firing of cannon, and hastened to bear the news of his success to Ferdinand and Isabella. Thousands crowded around him on his journey to court. The streets and windows were lined with people, and the Indians he had brought with him were looked at with as much wonder as if they had come from the moon. With no less wonder did they gaze at the strange scenes about them.

10. Remember the date of the discovery of America.—October 12, 1492.

QUESTIONS.—1. How did a ship of Columbus's time differ from one of the present day? For what was the round box on the mast used?—2. With how many ships did Columbus set out? What was thought of the voyage? How many men were obtained?

From what port, and when, did Columbus sail? How old was he?—3. Where did Columbus stop for repairs? When his men had been some days out, how did they begin to feel? What did they even talk of doing?—4. What promise did Columbus have to make? What signs of land soon appeared? When was land discovered? How did the sailors now feel?—5. Describe the land, as it appeared at daylight. What were seen on the shore? What did the natives take the ships to be?—6. Give an account of the landing of Columbus.—7. What was the land thus discovered? What name did Columbus give it? What did he call the natives, and why? What are the islands of this region still called?—8. What islands were next discovered by Columbus? What occurred at Haiti? What did Columbus take with him on his return?—9. What took place on the return voyage? What precautions did Columbus take? What was the result of the storm? How were Columbus and his companions received?—10. What was the date of the discovery of America?

LESSON IV.

LATER VOYAGES OF COLUMBUS.—CABOT.

1. The news of Columbus's discovery threw all Europe into excitement. Wonderful stories were told about the new land in the west. Many believed that gold grew on the trees, and that diamonds were as common there as stones in other countries. Those who had before laughed at Columbus, now thought that their fortunes would be made if they could only get to the land he had discovered. "To the west! To the west!" was the cry of every bold navigator that could fit out a vessel.

2. Columbus himself made three more voyages to the western world. On his third voyage, in 1498, he first reached the main land, near the mouth of the O-ri-no'-co, in South America.

3. Meanwhile murmurs arose among those he had brought out, because they did not find gold so plenty as they had expected. The enemies of Columbus, too, spread false reports about him in Spain. Moved by these stories, and forgetting all he had done, the

LESSON V.

BALBOA.—MAGELLAN.—CORTEZ.

1. The Pacific Ocean was discovered in 1513 by Bal-bo'-a, governor of a Spanish settlement on the Isthmus of Darien. Hearing of a vast body of water to the south, he raised about two hundred men, and with native guides set out to reach it. Balboa and his men wore heavy armor, and could hardly make their way through the pathless forests and over rocks and mountains. A fierce tribe of Indians opposed their progress; but, defeating these with the aid of their fire-arms and bloodhounds, they pushed on. Many, however, had to stop by the way from sickness and fatigue; and with less than half of his party Balboa found himself ascending the peak from the top of which the guides said that the great water could be seen.

2. When near the top, Balboa ordered his men to halt, and climbed alone to the summit. There he saw the mighty Pacific rolling away as far as eye could reach. His first act was to thank God for the discovery. He afterwards descended to the shore, and, with his sword in one hand and his country's flag in the other, wading out knee-deep into the water, took possession of it in the name of the King of Spain, and declared that he would defend it with his arms.

3. *Pacific* means *peaceful*. The ocean discovered by Balboa received this name on account of its freedom from storms compared with the Atlantic. It was so called by Ma-gel'-lan, a Portuguese, who was the first to sail a ship on its waters. He entered it through a strait at the south of South America, since called from him the Strait of Magellan.

4. Magellan lost his life on this voyage. One of his ships, however, continued to sail west, rounded the Cape of Good Hope, and

Balboa taking possession of the Pacific Ocean.

reached home after an absence of three years. This was the first vessel that ever sailed round the globe.—What did this voyage prove respecting the shape of the earth?

5. Next followed the conquest of Mexico, in 1519. Mexico was a vast empire. Its people were far more civilized than the natives in other parts of North America. They had laws and courts of

justice, public schools, splendid temples, and large cities. They tilled the ground, worked their rich mines of gold and silver, and were acquainted with many of the arts and sciences. Their Emperor lived in a magnificent palace in the city of Mexico. He was waited on by six hundred nobles. His dishes and goblets were of gold. He called himself lord of the whole world, and made the neighboring tribes pay him tribute. The Mexicans did not worship the true God, but bowed down to idols of wood and stone. To these false gods they cruelly sacrificed the captives that they took in war.

6. The Spaniards, who were now quite numerous in Cuba and the neighboring islands, heard of this rich empire, and resolved to conquer it. They raised about six hundred men, and placed at their head a brave but cruel man named Cortez. Sixteen of the party had horses, and a few were armed with muskets. The rest carried swords, spears, and bows. With this small force and ten cannon, Cortez set out to conquer a great empire containing several millions of people.

7. As soon as the Mexican Emperor heard that the Spaniards had landed, he sent messengers to them with rich presents, but with orders that they should leave the country. Cortez received the presents, but paid no attention to the orders. Having burned his ships, that his men might not think of returning, he pushed into the interior.

8. Before reaching the capital, several battles were fought with immense armies of natives; but the Spaniards were always successful. The poor natives were dismayed by the muskets and cannon, breathing forth fire and mowing down their ranks. They were also frightened by Cortez' horsemen, whom they took for horrible monsters, half men and half beasts. Horses had never before been seen on the American Continent.

9. After a great deal of hard fighting, in the course of which he was once driven out of the city with great loss, Cortez at last got possession of the capital, the Emperor, and the principal nobles. He treated his captives very cruelly. Gold was his great object; and he was wicked enough to stretch the poor Mexicans on beds of hot coals to make them tell where they had hidden their treasures. He put a great many to death, and subdued the whole nation. From this time Mexico remained a Spanish province for about three hundred years.

QUESTIONS.—1. By whom was the Pacific Ocean discovered? With how many men did Balboa start? What difficulties were encountered? How many of his men were disabled?—2. When near the top, what did Balboa do? What did he see? What was his first act? What did he afterwards do?—3. What does the word *pacific* mean? Why was the ocean so called? Who gave it this name? How did Magellan enter the Pacific?—4. What became of Magellan? What was done by one of his ships?—5. What conquest next followed? When? Give an account of the Mexicans and their Emperor. What did they worship?—6. What did the Spaniards resolve to do? What preparations did they make for conquering Mexico?—7. What did the Mexican Emperor do, when he heard the Spaniards had landed? What was done by Cortez?—8. What took place before the Spaniards reached the capital? What was the result of these battles? What frightened the natives?—9. After much hard fighting, what did Cortez succeed in doing? How did he treat his captives? How long did Mexico remain a Spanish province?

LESSON VI.

FRENCH DISCOVERIES.—DE SOTO.

1. Other countries now began to send out ships to the new world, as well as Spain and England. In 1524, a navigator in the service of the King of France, explored the coast from Carolina to Newfoundland. He called the whole region New France. Ten years afterwards, a Frenchman named Cartier [*car-te-ā'*] made sev-

eral voyages to America. He entered the River St. Lawrence, and sailed up to a large Indian village, which stood where Montreal has since been built. The Indians were at first very friendly, but he made them enemies by carrying off their chief.

2. Shortly after this, a number of Frenchmen sailed to the new world, and settled on the St. Lawrence River. They found it so cold and uninviting, however, that after passing one winter there they were glad to return. Several other settlements were attempted by the French in the south, but without success.

3. Meanwhile the Spaniards, eager for gold, which they heard was plenty in the interior of the country, were constantly sending out exploring parties. One of the most famous of these was led by a governor of Cuba, named De Soto. He landed on the coast of Florida, with six hundred men in complete armor. De Soto took with him a blacksmith's forge, so that when his weapons wore out he could make new ones. That his men might not want for food, he drove a great number of hogs before him through the woods. Thus prepared, and well furnished with horses and supplies, De Soto and his party set out on their journey of discovery.

4. For many months they wandered to and fro over what is now Alabama and Georgia. They met many Indians, who would have been friendly if the Spaniards had not, like Cortez, treated them cruelly. They were disappointed because they could not find any gold, and they wreaked their anger on the innocent natives. They robbed them of whatever they wanted, and for the slightest cause burned their villages, cut off their hands, and gave them to their bloodhounds to tear in pieces.

5. Such treatment provoked the Indians, and at last a battle was fought. The Spaniards, with the aid of their fire-arms and horses, were victorious, and killed a great many of the natives.

Some months afterwards, the Spaniards having seized on the village of a tribe in the north of what is now Mississippi, the natives revenged themselves by setting fire to their own wigwams in the night. De Soto lost in the flames many horses and hogs, most of his baggage, and eleven of his men.

6. Continuing his march, De Soto in a few days found himself on the bank of a mighty river now called the Mississippi. In the engraving, you see him and his men on a high bluff, gazing on the great stream they have discovered. The river is alive with canoes full of natives, who are hastening to bring presents to the strangers, not knowing how cruel they are.

7. De Soto was a proud man, and he would not go back unsuccessful. Hearing of gold in the northwest, he crossed the Mississippi and marched in that direction. Many weary miles he trav-

elled. His Indian guides led him into thick woods and dangerous swamps. To get rid of him, the tribes he visited would tell him wonderful stories about some other country a little farther on, where gold was plenty. Thus he was kept marching about, only to find himself deceived and disappointed.

8. De Soto's men were now dying around him from exposure and fatigue. He saw that his hopes of wealth and glory were vain, and became disheartened. A fever seized him, and he died with little comfort in his last hours. His men wrapped his body in a cloak, and, taking it out in a boat, sunk it at dead of night in the great Mississippi which he had discovered.

9. After De Soto's death, his men continued their wanderings. They first tried to reach Mexico by land, and made their way as far as the prairies of Texas. Then, ready to sink, they turned back to the Mississippi, and resolved to sail down to its mouth, and thence along the coast to some Spanish settlement. Every scrap of iron was used in making nails to hold their frail vessels together. After undergoing the severest hardships, about half of the party succeeded in reaching their countrymen. They had spent over four years in their weary wanderings.

QUESTIONS.—1. In 1524, who explored the coast of America? What name did he give the region he visited? Give an account of Cartier's discoveries. How did he treat the Indians?—2. Where did some Frenchmen attempt to settle? What made them return? Where were other settlements attempted by the French?—3. Meanwhile, what were the Spaniards doing? Who led a famous expedition? Where did De Soto land? How many men had he? What did he take with him?—4. Where did De Soto wander for many months? How did he treat the Indians?—5. What was the consequence of the Spaniards' cruelty? What was the result of the battle? How did a Mississippi tribe revenge themselves?—6. What great discovery was made by De Soto? Describe the scene in the engraving.—7. Where did De Soto next go, and why? How did the Indian tribes try to get rid of him?—8. In what condition did De Soto now find his men?

What befell De Soto himself? What was done with his corpse?—9. What did De Soto's men do after his death? How many reached their countrymen? How long had they been gone?

LESSON VII.

THE AMERICAN INDIANS.

1. We have said a great deal about the Indians; it is time that we describe them. Here is a picture of one. He is tall and straight. In his right hand is his pipe of peace. Around his neck is a collar ornamented with the claws of bears that he has killed. At his back he carries his tomahawk, his bow, and a quiver full of arrows. He wears moccasins on his feet, and deer-skin leggings. His head is bare; he has no hair except a single scalp-lock, adorned with feathers.

2. There were many different tribes of Indians in different parts of America; but they looked alike and led the same kind of life. They were all copper-colored, and hence have been called Red Men. Their hair was black, and very straight and coarse. In the north, they clothed themselves with skins; but in the south, where the climate was warmer, they wore little or no covering.

3. The Indian spent most of his time in the chase. He obtained his food by hunting and fishing, and raised nothing except a little maize or Indian corn. This the women were obliged to plant and cultivate. The warrior thought it beneath him to labor, and made his wife, or *squaw*, as he called her, do all the work. She put up

their hut, prepared their food, and when they moved from place to place even carried the baggage.

4. When the Indian was out hunting, or on the war-trail, he slept in the open air, with a fire burning beside him to frighten wild beasts away. At home he occupied a *wigwam*, or hut, such as is shown in the engraving. It was made by stretching bark or skins over poles stuck in the ground. Here you see the chief taking his ease, while his wife is cooking the dinner. The little chief is playing with his father's bow. The baby, or *pappoose*, strapped up to keep him still, is leaning against the side of the wigwam. An Indian woman often travelled miles with her pappoose fastened in this way on her back. The wigwams of different tribes were usually built together in villages.

Indian Wigwam.

5. The Indians generally, though cautious and suspicious, were friendly and hospitable. They would set before a stranger the best they had, and were grieved if he would not eat. If any one did them a favor, they would remember it for years, and return it when it was in their power. An Indian has been known to save the life of a white man who had given him food or drink so long before as to have forgotten all about it.

They remembered injuries also, and were unsparing in their revenge.

6. The Indians were constantly engaged in wars with each other. Arrayed in their war-paint, they collected in small parties under distinguished chiefs. They carried neither baggage nor provisions. Each man depended on the game that he could shoot by the way.

7. Their object was to surprise their enemies, to kill as many as possible, and escape unhurt. They never fought on an open field. Their movements were made as secretly as possible. The chief led the way, and each of the party trod noiselessly in his footsteps. To conceal their trail from the enemy, the last of the party would sometimes cover it with leaves. But it was hard to deceive an experienced foe in this way. The Indian could see and hear at a great distance, and observed little things that would escape the notice of a white man.

8. An enemy killed in battle was scalped at once. Without this, there was no glory in the victory. A distinguished chief could point to a dozen dried scalps hanging at his girdle or in his wigwam. All prisoners were either killed on the spot, or taken home in triumph. They were there sometimes adopted by the tribe in place of warriors that had fallen, but were more generally tortured.

9. A common mode of dealing with prisoners was to make them "run the gauntlet". Two long lines were formed, of men, women, and children, armed with clubs. The prisoner was placed at one end, and obliged to run to the other, unless before reaching it he sunk under the blows showered upon him as he passed.

10. They would sometimes fasten their captives to trees, and fling tomahawks at their heads, to see how near they could come, without striking them. At other times, they would fasten their victim to a stake, and pile up burning branches and fagots around

THEIR MODES OF BURIAL. 27

him. They would shoot blazing arrows into his flesh, and try to torment him in every way they could; while he, in spite of his sufferings, would neither flinch nor groan, but meet his fate bravely, singing his war-song, and boasting how many of their relations he had slain.

11. When an Indian warrior died, his knife and tomahawk, bow and arrows, and sometimes his favorite dog, were buried with him. They thought that in the other world he would need them, as he had done here. They buried the dead in different ways. Some erected a high platform, on which they placed the body in a kind of coffin. Others buried it in a sitting posture, or set it on the ground, and built over it a little house of bark. A mother would sometimes suspend the body of her dead child from the branch of a tree, and sing to it as it waved in the breeze. The graves of their fathers they defended with the greatest bravery.

12. The Indians believed that all men would live again after death: the bad, in a place of torment; but the good, in the happy hunting-grounds, where deer, buffaloes, and all kinds of game abounded. They did not worship idols, like the Mexicans. They believed in a Great Spirit, and prayed to Him for every thing they wanted.

QUESTIONS.—1. Describe the Indian represented in the engraving.—2. What is said of the different tribes? Why have the Indians been called Red Men? What kind of hair had they? How were they clothed in the north? How, in the south?—3. In what did the Indian spend most of his time? How did he obtain his food? What did he raise? What did the Indian squaw have to do?—4. How did the Indian sleep, when out hunting? At home, what did he occupy? How was the wigwam made? Describe the scene represented in the engraving.—5. How did the Indians treat strangers? What were they sure to remember?—6. In what were the Indians constantly engaged? When on a war-trail, on what did they depend for food?—7. What was their object in war? How did they move? How did they conceal their trail?—8. What was done to an enemy killed in battle? How were prisoners treated?—9. What common mode of dealing with prisoners is mentioned? What is meant by "running the gauntlet"?—10. How would they sometimes torture a captive? How would the captive bear these tortures?—11. What were buried with an Indian warrior? Why was this done? Describe the different modes of burying. What would a mother sometimes do with the corpse of her child?—12. What did the Indians believe respecting the state after death? To whom did they pray?

LESSON VIII.

THE FIRST SETTLEMENTS.

Though different parts of the country were explored, as we have seen, yet seventy years after the discovery of Columbus there was no settlement of white men within what is now the United States. The Spanish were the first to plant a permanent colony. In 1565, they founded St. Augustine [*aw-gus-teen'*], in Florida. This place, still known by the same name, is the oldest settlement in the United States.

2. Forty years later, a French colony settled in Nova Scotia. Soon afterwards, a Frenchman named Champlain planted a colony of his countrymen in Canada, on the spot where Quebec now stands. You remember there is a beautiful lake in the State of New York, called Champlain. It received its name from this

Frenchman, who discovered it while on an expedition against the Indians. The French at this time held the northern part of the continent, just as the Spaniards did the southern.

3. Between the possessions of the French and the Spanish was a large tract claimed by England. Sir Walter Raleigh, a favorite of Queen Elizabeth, undertook to colonize it. He sent out a party in two ships, which reached the coast of North Carolina. They found a rich and pleasant land, occupied by a friendly tribe. An Indian Queen entertained them on Roanoke Island. Persuading two natives to accompany them, they returned to England, and gave so glowing an account of the country they had visited, that the Virgin Queen, Elizabeth, was delighted, and named it in honor of herself, VIRGINIA.

4. Raleigh, thus encouraged, sent out a number of emigrants. They settled on the pleasant fields of Roanoke Island; but their governors were imprudent. One of them burned an Indian village, because a silver cup was stolen from his men. Another fell on a party of friendly Indians, thinking them to be enemies, and killed several before he found out his mistake. Such acts made the kind natives angry and revengeful. Some of the settlers became disheartened, and returned to England. The rest were killed.

5. Still Raleigh was not discouraged. He sent out more settlers to Roanoke, who laid out "the city of Raleigh". Their governor went back to England for supplies, and was absent two years. On his return to the island, there was not a white man to be seen. Whether they had been killed or carried off by the Indians, was never found out.

6. Sir Walter Raleigh's means were now spent, and he had to give up his attempts to colonize Virginia. Though he was afterwards beheaded on a charge of treason, he is regarded as one of

the greatest men of his day. The state of North Carolina has called its capital RALEIGH in his honor.

7. Raleigh was the first to introduce potatoes into Europe. He planted some on his Irish estates. Others obtained seed from him, and now potatoes are the chief food of the poor in Ireland. He brought over from America another thing, which the people of Europe could have done without,—and that is tobacco. He learned to smoke it from the Indians. One day his servant, who had never seen tobacco used, entering his master's room, found him surrounded with smoke, and thinking he was on fire dashed a mug of ale over him.

8. The first permanent English settlement was made in 1607, by a party under Captain Newport. They were sent out by a company to whom Virginia had been granted. Carried by a storm past Roanoke Island, where they meant to land, they entered a noble river, which they called after their King, THE JAMES. Some miles above its mouth, they chose a favorable spot, and laid out the city of Jamestown. This region belonged to Powhatan, a famous Indian chief, the head of thirty tribes. Some of the Indians did not like the white men's settling there. But Powhatan said, "Let them alone. They hurt you not. They only take a little waste land."

9. Newport soon returned to England. Hardly was he gone when the settlers were attacked with sickness. At one time only ten were able to stand. In a few weeks but half the party were left alive, and they were seized with despair. They would no doubt all have perished, had they not at this crisis placed Captain John Smith at their head.

10. Smith was a brave and wise man. He soon had things in a better state. He made the idle work, and prevented the timid from

sailing away, as they had intended to do. He explored the surrounding country, and kept in check the natives, who were becoming suspicious and unfriendly.

QUESTIONS.—1. For how many years was there no permanent settlement in what is now the United States? Who planted the first permanent colony? When and where?— 2. What settlement was made forty years afterwards? Where was a colony planted by Champlain? What received its name from Champlain? What part of the continent did the French hold? The Spanish?—3. Who claimed the tract between the French and the Spanish possessions? Who undertook to colonize it? Give an account of the first expedition sent out by Raleigh. What name was given to the region, and why?—4. Where did the second party sent out by Raleigh settle? What acts of imprudence were committed by their governors?—What was the consequence?—5. What did Raleigh next do? What city was laid out? What became of this colony?—6. What became of Raleigh? How is he regarded? What city has been named in his honor?—7. What useful article did Raleigh introduce into Europe? What else? What anecdote is related of his servant?—8. When and by whom was the first permanent English settlement made? Where did this party mean to land? Where did they land? What city did they lay out? To whom did this region belong? How did some of the Indians feel towards the English? What did Powhatan say?—9. What happened soon after Newport's return to England? What saved the colony?—10. What kind of a man was Captain Smith? What measures did he take?

LESSON IX.

CAPTAIN JOHN SMITH.

1. Captain Smith's early life was full of adventures. Running away from home in his youth, he helped the Dutch fight for their freedom. But he soon got tired of this, and one dark night he deserted, and made his way to France. Then he went to Egypt. Wherever there was anything wonderful to see, he wandered.

2. On one of his voyages, he acted rudely towards some of his fellow-passengers, and they threw him overboard. He came near drowning; but saved himself by swimming to a rocky island,

where he stayed until a passing vessel took him off. Next we find him in Hungary, fighting the Turks hand to hand, like the knights of old. At last, being wounded in a skirmish, he was taken prisoner and sold as a slave.

3. Smith was now carried off hundreds of miles into a dreary country. He was loaded with chains, and treated harshly. So he resolved to escape. Seizing his chance, he rose against his oppressor, and mounting a horse, fled through pathless forests to Russia. Hence, after some further adventures, he made his way back to England, in time to join Newport's party.

Captain John Smith.

4. While out on one of his exploring expeditions in Virginia, Smith was suddenly attacked by Indians. He had ordered his men to stay by the boat while he went out to reconnoitre; but they wandered off, and were killed by the savages. After slaying three of his enemies, Smith, while trying to escape, sunk in a swamp and had to yield. Even then the Indians were afraid to touch him till he had thrown away his arms. He would now have lost his life, if he had not understood the character of the Indians. Taking his compass out of his pocket, he showed them how the needle always points north, and told them about the shape of the Earth and the heavenly bodies.

5. To increase the wonder of the savages, Smith told them that

the next day they would find some articles that he named, in a certain place in the forest. He then wrote to his countrymen at Jamestown to put the articles there. They did so; and when the Indians, who did not understand his writing, saw every thing turn out as he had said, they began to look on him as more than man. They carried him around to their different villages in triumph, and at last brought him to their chief, Powhatan.

6. Here a solemn council was held, and it was determined

Pocahontas saving Captain Smith.

that Smith should be put to death. His head was laid on a large stone to receive the fatal blow. A fierce savage stood beside him, war-club in hand. Just as he was about to strike, Po-ca-hon'-tas, a gentle Indian girl of twelve years, ran forward, threw her arms about the prisoner, and with tears besought the savages to spare his life. She was the daughter of Powhatan, and the favorite of the whole tribe. Smith had amused her, during his captivity, by making her toys, and telling her about the wonders of nature. She had become fond of the stranger, and now tried to save him.

7. Moved by the tears of Pocahontas, the Indians spared Captain Smith. They even treated him kindly, and let him go back to Jamestown with promises of friendship. Pocahontas continued the firm friend of the English. She often visited them, bringing baskets of corn to relieve their wants. Once, when the Indians had formed a plot to surprise and murder all the whites, she came through the woods by night at the risk of her own life, and warned them to be on their guard.

8. On his return to Jamestown, Smith found the colonists reduced to forty men, and these were on the point of leaving in despair. He made them remain, and soon after Newport arrived with fresh settlers and supplies. Some of the new comers were goldsmiths; and, seeing some glittering sand near the town, they fancied it must be gold dust. Newport was foolish enough to load his vessel with this worthless sand, and carry it to England.

QUESTIONS.—1. Relate some of Captain Smith's early adventures.—2. What took place on one of his voyages? What do we next find him doing?—3. How was Smith treated during his captivity? Give an account of his escape.—4. What befell Smith, while out on one of his exploring expeditions? How did he save himself from immediate death?—5. How did Captain Smith increase the wonder of the savages? What did they do with him?—6. What took place when they reached Powhatan's village?

How was Smith saved? Why did Pocahontas want to save Smith?—7. After sparing his life, how did the Indians treat Captain Smith? What services did Pocahontas render the English?—8. In what condition did Smith find affairs at Jamestown? Who soon after arrived? What mistake did some of the new comers fall into?

LESSON X.

THE VIRGINIA COLONY.

1. Smith could not remain idle. In 1608, he set out on a voyage of discovery in an open boat. He explored Chesapeake Bay, and several large rivers that flow into it. He traded with the Indians, and made a map of the whole region he visited. Soon after his return, Newport again arrived with more settlers. But they were not used to hard work. So they did the colony very little good.

2. Soon after this, Lord Delaware was appointed governor of Virginia, and nine vessels were sent out with supplies and men. Most of the ships arrived safe at Jamestown; but the one that contained the leaders of the party was wrecked, and it was months before they reached the colony. Meanwhile Smith had hard work to manage affairs. Those who had arrived last were idle and quarrelsome, and said he had no right to order them about.

3. There was danger, too, of starving. Powhatan, alarmed by the increasing numbers of the English, said he had no corn to spare, and would neither give nor sell them any. But Smith knew better than this. So, taking some large blue beads with him, he went to see Powhatan. Showing them as if by accident, he told the chief that in his country none but kings were allowed to wear such ornaments. When Powhatan heard this, he gladly gave several hundred bushels of corn for a few of the beads. Another

time, he gave nearly a hundred bushels of corn for a little copper kettle. Do you think it was right for Smith to impose on the simple Indian in this way, even to save the lives of his countrymen?

4. In spite of all his difficulties, Captain Smith managed the colony well, till he was injured by an explosion of gunpowder. Then he had to return to England. No sooner was he gone than every thing went wrong. The colonists would not work any more, but called on the Indians to keep them supplied with corn. The Indians refused, and plotted together to destroy the whites. Several small parties were cut off. Some of the colonists seized a vessel and sailed away. The rest almost died of famine. Long was this period remembered as *the starving time.*

5. The arrival of Lord Delaware himself, with men and provisions, alone saved the colony. Under Delaware and his successors, Virginia flourished. Cattle and hogs were introduced from Europe. Tobacco was cultivated and exported to England. As coin was scarce, tobacco passed for money.

6. Thus far very few women had come over to America. In 1620, to make the colonists attached to their new country, the London Company sent over ninety young women. These were soon married to the settlers, who gave a hundred pounds of tobacco apiece for the expense of bringing them over. The next year more were sent out. There was soon many a pleasant home on the fertile fields of Virginia.

7. Perhaps you would like to know what became of Pocahontas. This lovely Indian girl, when about eighteen years old, was betrayed into the hands of a party of Englishmen. They refused to give her up unless Powhatan would ransom her. Instead of doing this, the old chief resolved on war. At this crisis, a young planter named Rolfe, who had fallen in love with the beautiful Indian, of-

fered her his hand in marriage. She accepted it, gave up her former religion, and became a Christian. Powhatan approved of the marriage, and ever from that time remained faithful to the English.

8. Rolfe afterwards took his wife to England. She was received with much kindness. Rooms were given her in the palace, and the noblest in the land flocked to see her. Among others, came her old friend, Captain Smith, whose life she had saved. All admired her winning ways. But the climate of England was too cold for her. She was about returning to Virginia, when she died, leaving an only son. Several Virginia families trace their descent to this Indian princess.

9. Powhatan sent one of his warriors to England with Pocahontas, to see the country and find out how many people were there. When they reached England, this Indian got a long stick, thinking he would number the inhabitants by making a notch on it for every one he saw. He soon had to stop. On his return, Powhatan asked him many questions, and among the rest how many people he had seen in England. "Count the stars in the sky," he replied, "the leaves on the trees, or the sands on the shore, for such is the number of the English."

QUESTIONS.—1. What did Captain Smith do in 1608? What took place shortly after his return?—2. Who was soon afterwards appointed governor? How many vessels were sent out? What happened to one of these? Who managed affairs till the leaders of the party arrived? What difficulties did he labor under?—3. What other danger was there? How did Smith manage to get some corn from Powhatan?—4. What obliged Captain Smith to return to England? What was the consequence of his return? What was this period called?—5. What saved the colony? What was the state of affairs under Delaware? What passed for money?—6. In 1620, what was done by the London company, to make the colonists attached to their new country? What was the price of a wife?—7. What became of Pocahontas?—8. Where did Rolfe take his wife? How was she received? What effect had the climate of England on her?—9. What anecdote is related of one of Powhatan's warriors?

LESSON XI.

DUTCH SETTLEMENTS.—HENRY HUDSON.

1. The next settlement was made in what is now the state of New York, by the Dutch. This nation traded largely with the East Indies. They thought that the voyage thither would be much shortened, if a passage could be found from the Atlantic Ocean to the Pacific, north of America. No such passage has ever been found, because the land extends far north to where the ocean is frozen by the intense cold. But the Dutch did not know this; so they sent out a navigator named Henry Hudson, to discover "a north-west passage".

2. The chief river in New York, you remember, is the Hudson. It is so called from this same navigator, who discovered it. Striking the coast of Maine, Hudson sailed south as far as Virginia without finding the passage he was in search of. Then turning back and closely examining the coast, he discovered an inlet between New Jersey and Long Island. He entered it, and soon found himself in what is now the noble harbor of New York.

3. The island on which the city of New York stands, is called Manhattan. This is an Indian word, meaning *the place of drunkenness*. I will tell you why it was so called. When Hudson's ship was coming up the bay, some Indians who were fishing saw it in the distance, and could not make out what it was. They called together their companions from far and near, and watched the strange object as it approached. Some thought it was a floating wigwam; others, that it was a big fish. At last they concluded it was a huge canoe, containing the Manitou, or Good Spirit, who was about to visit them.

4. A great feast was prepared, and the chiefs engaged in a grand

dance. At last the ship stopped, a boat was lowered, and Henry Hudson, dressed in red, entered it with a number of his men. Now they were sure the Manitou was come, and formed a circle to receive him.

5. When Hudson reached the land, he saluted the natives, and then produced a bottle of liquor. After drinking a glass himself, he poured out another, and handed it to the nearest chief. Afraid to drink it, the Indian only smelled the liquor, and passed it to the next, who did the same. Thus the glass passed around the whole circle, and was about to be handed back untasted, when one of the chiefs, fearing that the Manitou would be angry, took it and said he would drink it, no matter what the consequences might be.

6. No sooner had he drained the glass than he began to stagger, and at last he fell to the ground. His friends thought he was dead; but he soon got up again, and declared he had never before felt so happy. They were all now eager to try the wonderful " firewater ", and it ended in all the natives' getting drunk.

7. The next day, Hudson distributed some beads, stockings, and axe-heads, among his new friends. They were delighted with these presents, but did not know how to use them. The next time the Dutch visited the spot, they saw that the Indians had turned the stockings into tobacco-pouches, and strung the heavy axe-heads around their necks as ornaments.

8. Hudson sailed up the river till it became so shallow that he could go no farther. One of his boats ascended beyond where Albany now stands. After holding friendly intercourse with several native tribes, he sailed down again to the mouth, and thence back to Europe, to give an account of his discoveries. The next year he made another voyage. Sailing farther north, he discovered Hudson Bay, but lost his life in its icy waters.

9. The Dutch followed up Hudson's discovery by sending out trading vessels to the region he had visited. They obtained large quantities of beaver-skins and other furs from the Indians, in exchange for beads, knives, and hatchets. This was found so profitable that forts were built at different points to protect the traders. One of these was erected on Manhattan Island, in 1614. A few huts were put up around it, and the name of New Amsterdam was given to the settlement. Such was the origin of the great city of New York. The whole region was called by the Dutch New Netherlands.

10. The Dutch were a quiet, honest people. They loved to smoke their pipes, and talked no more than they could help. They paid the Indians for their land, though they made good bargains, and got it very cheap. The whole island of Manhattan, now worth millions upon millions, cost them only twenty-four dollars. Wherever money was to be made by traffic with the natives, they established posts; and their traders soon spread out on Long Island, Staten Island, and New Jersey. But it was not till 1621 that families came over to settle in New Netherlands.

QUESTIONS.—1. Where and by whom was the next settlement made? Why did the Dutch want to find "a north-west passage"? Whom did they send out?—2. What was called after the navigator Hudson? Give an account of Hudson's voyage.—3. What is the name of the island on which the city of New York stands? What does this word mean? What did the Indians think when they saw Hudson's ship approaching?—4, 5, 6. Tell the story about Hudson's meeting with the Indians. Why, after this, did they call the place Manhattan?—7. What did Hudson give the Indians? What use did they make of these gifts?—8. How high did Hudson's ship ascend the river? How far did one of his boats go? What did Hudson then do? What discovery did he afterwards make? What was the fate of Hudson?—9. How did the Dutch follow up Hudson's discovery? In what did they trade? How did they protect the traders? What was the origin of the great city of New York? What was it first called? What was the whole region called?—10. What kind of a people were the Dutch? How much did they give for Manhattan Island? Where did they establish posts? Where did their traders spread out? When did families come over to New Netherlands?

LESSON XII.

THE PILGRIM FATHERS.

1. Captain John Smith, in one of his exploring voyages, visited the coast of what is now Maine and Massachusetts. To this northern region he gave the name of NEW ENGLAND. It was first permanently settled in 1620, by a party from England, who are often spoken of as the Pilgrim Fathers. They belonged to a religious sect called Puritans, who were ill treated in England because they wished to worship God in their own way.

2. A number of Puritan families determined to emigrate to America, that they might enjoy their religion unmolested. One hundred persons embarked on a little vessel called the Mayflower. They meant to settle near the Hudson River; but a long and stormy voyage brought them to the dreary shore of Cape Cod, on the Massachusetts coast.

3. Parties were sent out to explore the coast. They found nothing but some Indian graves and a small heap of corn. The ground was covered with snow, and many took violent colds, from which they afterwards died. A boat was then despatched with some of the leading men, to sail along the coast and find a good place for landing.

4. Bitterly cold the little party found it. The spray froze on their coats, and made them as stiff and bright as if they had been of steel. Once, when they had landed, some Indians came near, and raising the terrible war-whoop discharged a volley of arrows at

them; but the sound of the Pilgrims' muskets soon put the savages to flight. Resuming their voyage, they were overtaken by a violent storm and almost wrecked. They found shelter, however, on an island. There was a good harbor in the main land near by; and, as the country seemed to be more fertile than any they had before seen, they determined to land there, and sent for their companions on the Mayflower.

5. The landing of the Pilgrims took place on the 21st of December, 1620. The day is still kept by the people of New England.

They gave the name of Plymouth to the place they founded. It is on the eastern coast of Massachusetts. Here you have a picture of the Puritans, with their wives and children, landing on the bleak snow-covered shore.

6. The Pilgrims at once commenced building huts. But they had been exposed so much that many were taken ill. Six of their number died in December, and at one time almost every person in the settlement was stretched on a sick bed. Yet they kept stout hearts and put their trust in God.

7. The houses of the Puritans were built of rough logs. They had nothing but long grass with which to cover their roofs. One night in January, two of the party, Brown and Goodman, went out into the woods to gather some of this grass. On their return, they lost their way. Night was near at hand, and, to add to their trouble, a heavy snow-storm set in.

8. After trying in vain to find their way back, they sat down under the shelter of a large rock, and prepared to spend the night there. But before long the wind commenced howling among the branches, and in their fright they fancied it was the roaring of a lion. They knew not that there were no lions in America, and so they climbed a tree for safety. But there they were exposed to the cold wind, which pierced their clothes and made them shiver. Finding that they would freeze unless they kept in motion, they came down from the tree and walked round and round it as fast as they could till daylight.

9. Glad were the two wanderers when morning appeared. They lost no time in pursuing their way, and, after walking fast or running all day, they succeeded in reaching Plymouth in the evening. Their companions, having searched for them without success, had given them up for lost, and supposed that they had been killed or carried off by Indians. Long did Brown and Goodman re-

member the roaring of the lion and that freezing night in the woods.

QUESTIONS.—1. Who gave New England its name? When and by whom was New England first permanently settled? To what religious sect did the Pilgrim Fathers belong?—2. Why did the Puritans come to America? How many came at first? On what vessel? Where did they mean to settle? What part of the coast did they reach?—3. What was found by the exploring parties sent out? What was the consequence of their exposure? What did the Puritans finally do?—4. Relate the adventures of this exploring party. What did they at last find?—5. When did the Pilgrims land? What did they call the place they founded? Where is Plymouth situated? What do you see in the engraving?—6. What befell the Pilgrims after their landing?—7. Of what were the houses of the Puritans built? With what did they cover them? What happened one night in January?—8, 9. Tell the story about Brown and Goodman.

LESSON XIII.

THE PLYMOUTH COLONY.

1. The winter was gloomy enough for the Puritans. They suffered much from hardship and sickness. By April half their number had died. But the weather now grew mild. Birds began to appear. The fields became green. The sick soon got better.

2. The country around Plymouth, though deserted when the Pilgrims settled there, showed signs of having been inhabited before. Smoke was seen afar off several times through the winter, and parties were sent out to find the Indians from whose fires it came, and open a friendly intercourse with them. They did not succeed; but early in the spring a single Indian entered the town. The settlers were surprised, as he approached, to hear him say, "Welcome, Englishmen!" He had learned a little English from previous voyagers.

3. The name of this Indian was Sam'-o-set. He told the white

men that he belonged to a tribe that lived about five days' journey off. That they were welcome to the land where they had settled, for there was no one else to claim it. That, several years before, the Indians who had lived there had been swept off by a pestilence. About this pestilence a curious story is told.

4. It seems that, a few years before the Pilgrims landed, a French ship went ashore on Cape Cod, and the Indians cruelly put to death nearly all on board of her. One of the Frenchmen, who was spared, remained some time with the Indians as a captive. One day he told them that the Great Spirit would punish them for having killed his countrymen, and would give their land to others. But they laughed at him, and asked whether he supposed that his Great Spirit could destroy so powerful a tribe as theirs. He replied that, if God wanted to destroy them, He would easily find a way. Soon after this a fatal disease broke out, which swept off nearly the whole tribe. The few that remained were killed by a hostile nation. This was the reason why the Puritans had seen so many graves, but no living Indians.

5. The Pilgrims treated Samoset kindly, and soon after his chief, Mas-sas'-o-it, came to pay them a visit. They received Massasoit with great respect. They presented him two knives and a copper chain, and gave his brother a pot of "strong water", and some biscuits and butter. A treaty was made, and Massasoit and his tribe always remained faithful friends of the white men.

6. Two of the Puritans soon afterwards returned Massasoit's visit. They found the chief very sick, and his medicine-men trying to cure him with hideous noises and foolish dances. Turning them out of the wigwam, one of the Puritans gave the chief some simple remedy, and restored him to health. He never forgot this kindness.

7. All the Indians, however, were not so friendly. A tribe

that was at war with Massasoit, sent to the Puritans a bundle of arrows wrapped in a rattle-snake's skin. This was their way of declaring war. The Puritan governor sent back the skin filled with powder and balls. The Indians thought the bullets were charms, and were so frightened that they concluded to let the white men alone. The Pilgrims, however, expecting an attack, put up a row of stakes, or palisades, as they were called, around their settlement.

8. For some time the Puritans continued to suffer, especially from hunger. They could not raise enough to support them. There were fish in the bay, but they had no boats or nets with which to take them. Even two years after their arrival, they often went to bed at night without a bit of food for the morning. If a few of their old friends joined them, a lobster or a piece of fish, without any bread or anything else but a cup of water, was all they had to offer them.

9. But in three or four years things were better. Each settler had his own tract of land. They worked hard, and corn was raised in abundance. More of their own faith came over from England. In 1630, their number had increased to three hundred. From this time the colony flourished.

QUESTIONS.—1. What kind of a winter did the Puritans pass? What was the state of things in April?—2. What signs did the country around Plymouth show? What was seen several times in the winter? Give an account of Samoset's visit.—3. What did Samoset tell the white men?—4. What story is related about this pestilence?—5. How did the Pilgrims treat Samoset? Who soon after visited them? What did they present to Massasoit? What did they give his brother? What was the consequence?—6. What service did two of the Puritans afterwards render to Massasoit?—7. What warlike message did the Puritans receive? How did they answer it? What was the result? What precaution did the Pilgrims take?—8. From what did the Puritans suffer at first? When their friends joined them, what did they have to offer them?—9. In three or four years, what was the state of the colony? How many Puritans did it contain in 1630?

LESSON XIV.

OTHER NEW ENGLAND COLONIES.

1. MASSACHUSETTS BAY.—In 1630, a large company of English Puritans, having obtained a grant of land on Massachusetts Bay, north of Plymouth, came out and founded Cambridge, Boston, and other places. They formed what was called the Massachusetts Bay Colony. Though these settlers, like the rest, suffered much at first from cold and hunger, they soon began to prosper. Mills were built, and trade commenced with the other colonies. Boston is now, you remember, the capital of Massachusetts, and the largest city in New England. Here is a map of the eastern part of Massachusetts. See if you can find Cape Cod—Plymouth—Boston—Salem.

2. RHODE ISLAND.—The people of Salem had a young preacher named Roger Williams. His belief was somewhat different from that of the other Puritan ministers; but he claimed that he had a right to worship in his own way, and preach what he thought was the Bible truth. This, however, the people of Massachusetts Bay would not tolerate; and so they determined to send him back to England.

3. Hearing of their intentions, Roger Williams fled from Salem into the wilderness. He resolved to find some place where he could

enjoy that freedom which the Puritans denied him. More than three months he wandered amid snow and rain, without either bread or bed. At last he reached some Indian wigwams, where he was kindly received. He bought of the Indians a tract on Narragansett Bay, and commenced a settlement. Grateful for God's mercy, he called this place Providence. Turn to the map on page 47, and point out Providence, the first settlement in Rhode Island.

4. There is a beautiful island in Narragansett Bay, which the  Indians called the Isle of Peace. Soon after Providence was founded, another party that had difficulties with the Puritans of Massachusetts Bay, bought this island of the Indians, and settled on it. They called it the Isle of Rhodes. Near its southern shore was a curious old tower, shown in the engraving. No one could tell who built it. Near this tower the city of Newport was founded.

5. NEW HAMPSHIRE.—Settlements were made in what is now the state of New Hampshire, as early as 1623. A number of trading and fishing posts were afterwards established there. These settlements, at their own request, were received into the Massachusetts Bay Colony. But, after about forty years, they were formed into a separate province by the King of Great Britain, under the name of New Hampshire.

6. CONNECTICUT.—The Connecticut (or Long River, as the name means in the Indian language) was discovered by the Dutch of New Amsterdam. They built a fort where Hartford now stands, and opened a profitable trade with the Indians. But after a time

the people of Plymouth and Massachusetts Bay heard of this long river, whose waters were filled with fish, and whose banks abounded in beaver and otter. One day in the year 1633, the traders at the Dutch fort were surprised to see a little vessel come sailing up the river. They wanted to keep this pleasant country to themselves. So, loading a cannon, they hailed the vessel, and told the captain to stop, or they would fire on him.

7. The little vessel belonged to John Holmes. He had come from Plymouth to settle in the valley of the Connecticut, and brought with him the frame of a house to put up where he should land. He was not afraid of the Dutch or their cannon. So, since the wind was fair, he took no notice of their threats, but kept on his way. He passed the fort in safety, and settled a few miles higher up, at a place now called Windsor.

8. It did not take long for reports concerning the fair valley of the Connecticut to reach England. A great lord obtained a grant of it, and a party of settlers was sent over. They built a fort at the mouth of the river, and called it Saybrook.

QUESTIONS.—1. When and by whom was the Massachusetts Bay colony established? What places were founded? What has Boston since become?—2. Who was the founder of Rhode Island? Where was Roger Williams settled? Why did the people of Massachusetts Bay want to send him back to England?—3. How did Roger Williams escape being sent back to England? What did he resolve to do? Give an account of his wanderings. Where and how did he obtain some land? What did he call his settlement? —4. What other settlement was soon after made? What was found on the Isle of Rhodes? What city was founded near this tower?—5. When was New Hampshire first settled? With what colony were these settlements first united? After forty years what was done with them?—6. What does the word *Connecticut* mean? By whom was the Connecticut River discovered? Where did the Dutch build a fort? Who heard of this pleasant river? What were the Dutch surprised to see one day? What did they do?—7. To whom did the vessel belong? Where was it from? What did Holmes do? Where did he settle?—8. Where and by whom was Saybrook founded?

LESSON XV.

CONNECTICUT.—THE PEQUOD WAR.

1. Connecticut, as we learned in the last lesson, was first permanently settled at Windsor, by John Holmes. Two years afterwards, a party from Massachusetts Bay determined to settle there. They went over land, driving their cattle before them, through woods that neither cattle nor white men had ever before traversed. But they started too late. The river was frozen before they arrived. Their cattle perished, and they suffered much through the winter from want of food.

Puritans emigrating from Massachusetts to Connecticut.

2. The next summer, another party of about one hundred men, women, and children, set out from Boston for the valley of the Connecticut. They lived mostly on the milk of their cows, which they took with them. Moving slowly along, they were nearly a fortnight in completing a journey which can now be made by railroad in three or four hours. They arrived safe, and founded Hartford and Wethersfield.

3. Connecticut was inhabited by many powerful tribes of Indians. Among these were the Pequods, who lived in what is now the south-eastern part of the state, near the mouth of the Thames [*tamez*] River. When the Pequods saw the white men spreading over their pleasant hunting-grounds, they were filled with jealousy and alarm; and the whites, seeing how the Indians felt, distrusted them in turn. Up to this time there had been peace between the whites and Indians; but this suspicion soon produced war.

4. One day, a trader, sailing off the coast, saw a boat which he knew belonged to one of the settlers named Oldham. It was full of Indians, and he suspected there was something wrong. So, although he had only two boys with him, he made for the boat. The Indians were frightened when they saw him, and as he approached they jumped over into the water. The trader went on board, and under a fishing-net he found Oldham's body, all mangled and bleeding.

5. The people of New England determined to punish the murderers. A body of men started for the Pequod villages. The Indians had fled, but there were their wigwams and corn-fields. Setting fire to these, the settlers laid waste the country far and wide. This roused the Pequods to a bloody revenge. Dividing into small parties, they surrounded solitary houses, cut off travellers, shot down the men as they worked in the fields, and scalped women and children at their own firesides. They spared none.

6. Resolving to cut off all the English settlers, the Pequods tried to get another tribe, the Nar-ra-gan'-setts, to join them. When the people of Boston heard of this, they were greatly frightened. Knowing that Roger Williams, whom they had driven out shortly before, was much beloved by the Narragansetts, they sent to him, begging that he would dissuade his friends from joining the Pequods. This good man, on receiving their message, set out alone in his canoe, in a violent storm, for the Narragansett village. He found the Pequod chiefs already there; but he pleaded so earnestly, that, after wavering several days, the Narragansetts refused to join the Pequods, and declared themselves friends of the English.

7. The settlers now sent a body of men against the Pequods. Reaching one of their forts just before sun-rise, they surprised its inmates, and set fire to their wigwams. They then formed a ring around the wigwams, and, as the flames drove the Indians out, shot them down without mercy. Six hundred Pequods perished in an hour. The next morning, the rest of the tribe, who had been at another fort, came in sight and renewed the battle. They fought bravely, but were defeated by the English. The few that survived were pursued from place to place, and the whole tribe was destroyed.

8. In 1638, the year after the Pequod War, New Haven was founded, as a distinct colony, by a company of Puritans from England. The new colonists adopted the Bible as their only rule of public action.

9. The New England colonies grew and flourished. In 1643, they contained over fifty villages. Threatened at this time by the Indians, and also by the Dutch and French, they thought it best to combine for their mutual protection in case of war. Accordingly, Plymouth, Massachusetts Bay, Connecticut, and New Haven, form-

ed an alliance under the name of "The United Colonies of New England". This league lasted forty years, and was of great benefit to all.

QUESTIONS.—1. When and by whom was Connecticut first permanently settled? Two years afterwards, who went there? What befell this party from Massachusetts Bay?—2. What took place the next summer? On what did the emigrants live? How long did it take them to make the journey? What places did they found?—3. By whom was the greater part of Connecticut inhabited? Where did the Pequods live? What excited their jealousy? What was the consequence?—4. How was the murder of Oldham discovered?—5. How did the people of New England punish the murderers? What was the consequence?—6. Whom did the Pequods try to rouse against the English settlers? How did the English prevent them from succeeding?—7. What measures were next taken by the settlers? Give an account of the battle with the Pequods. What took place the next morning? What became of the few that survived?—8. When was New Haven founded? By whom? What did the settlers of New Haven adopt as their rule of public action?—9. In 1643, how many villages did the New England colonies contain? What alliance was formed in this year? How long did this league last?

LESSON XVI.

MARYLAND.—DELAWARE.—NEW JERSEY.

1. MARYLAND.—The next colony founded was Maryland. The region now so called was granted by the King of England to George Calvert, Lord Baltimore. Calvert desired to establish a colony where all might enjoy civil and religious freedom. His charter provided that the English government should not tax the colony or interfere with its affairs. The tract thus granted was called Maryland in honor of Henrietta Maria, the Queen of England.

2. Lord Baltimore died before he could plant his colony; but his son, Cè-cil Calvert, succeeded to the grant. In 1634, he sent over from England two hundred emigrants. They sailed up the Potomac River, which separates Maryland from Virginia, bought

some land from the natives, and built a little village. They gave the Indians knives, hoes, and axes; and the Indian women in return taught them how to make corn-bread and johnny-cake.

3. The settlers of Maryland did not suffer, like those who founded the other colonies. They arrived at a favorable season, and were helped by the people of Virginia. They were free and happy, and numbers joined them from England. Their only trouble was caused by a man named Clayborne, who, before their arrival, had established a trading-post within their boundaries. He stirred up several rebellions, but was at last put down. Baltimore, now the largest city in Maryland, was named after the founder of this colony.

4. DELAWARE.—Delaware was next founded, in 1638, by a company of Swedes and Finns. The Swedes are the inhabitants of Sweden, and the Finns of Finland,—two countries in the north of Europe. Though these nations had made no discoveries in the new world, they wanted to have a colony there, and fitted out a party of emigrants. Landing on the shore of Delaware Bay, the Swedes bought a tract from the Indians, and gave it the name of New Sweden. They erected several forts, and were soon joined by more of their countrymen.

5. Several years before the Swedes arrived, a party of Dutch from New Netherlands had settled in this region. They had been cut off by the Indians; yet now, when the Dutch saw strangers taking possession, they claimed the country on the ground that they had been the first to occupy it. A quarrel thus arose, which resulted (in 1655) in the conquest of New Sweden by the Dutch. The name was afterwards changed to Delaware.

6. The Dutch of New Netherlands had gone on trading and prospering, though for a time they suffered much from a war with the Indians, provoked by the cruelty of one of their governors.

Soon after this, Stuyvesant [*sti'-ve-sant*], a gallant old soldier who had lost a leg in the wars, became governor. It was under him that New Sweden was conquered.

7. While Stuyvesant was governor, the King of England granted the whole tract occupied by the Dutch to his brother, the Duke of York. Of course it was not his to grant, but he did not mind that. A powerful fleet was sent out to take possession. When the English arrived off New Amsterdam, they summoned Stuyvesant to surrender. But he boldly tore their letter to pieces, and, taking his station on the battery, prepared to fire on them as they approached.

8. Upon this, the people of New Amsterdam told Stuyvesant that if he fought the English he would have to do it alone. He had kept them down too much. So now they thought they would be just as well off under the English as they had ever been, and they refused to stand by their old governor. Brave as he was, therefore, he had to surrender. All the Dutch possessions, including what had been New Sweden, thus passed without the firing of a shot into the hands of the English.

9. This took place in 1664. The English were now masters of the whole Atlantic coast from Maine to Florida. In honor of the Duke of York, both the settlement of New Amsterdam and the whole colony of New Netherlands, after their conquest by the English, were called NEW YORK.

10. NEW JERSEY.—We have already seen that some of the Dutch traders had spread out west of the Hudson, and founded several villages. When the Duke of York gained possession of his grant, he gave this part of it to two of his friends, who called it New Jersey. They promised an unusual degree of freedom to all who would settle there, and the consequence was that New Jersey became rapidly peopled.

QUESTIONS.—1. What was the next colony founded? To whom was the region now called Maryland granted? What did Calvert desire? What did his charter provide? Why was this tract called Maryland?—2. By whom was a colony planted in Maryland? When? Where did they build a village? What did they give the Indians? What did the Indian women teach them?—3. What is said of the settlers of Maryland? By whom was their only trouble caused? What is the largest city in Maryland? After whom was it named?—4. When was Delaware founded? By whom? Who are the Swedes? The Finns? Where did they land? How did they obtain a tract? What did they call it? What did they erect?—5. Who disputed the right of the Swedes to this region? On what ground? What was the result? To what was the name of New Sweden changed? —6. From what did the Dutch of New Netherlands suffer for a time? Under whom was New Sweden conquered?—7. While Stuyvesant was governor, what grant was made by the King of England? What was the consequence? When the English fleet arrived, what did Stuyvesant do?—8. How did the people of New Amsterdam feel on the subject? Why was this? What followed?—9. When did the English make this conquest? What now belonged to them? To what did they change the names of New Amsterdam and New Netherlands?—10. What was the origin of New Jersey? What caused it to become rapidly peopled?

LESSON XVII.

KING PHILIP'S WAR.

1. For some years after the Pequod War, the New England colonies had no trouble with the Indians. But in 1675 King Philip's War broke out, which at first threatened to sweep off every white settler in Massachusetts. Philip was the son of Massasoit, who had been the friend of the English. He was the chief of the Wampa-no'-ags, who lived in what is now the state of Rhode Island, east of Narragansett Bay. Find their country on the map on page 47. The Narragansetts, you will see, lived on the opposite side of the bay.

2. The whites had now spread out very much. The Indians, seeing what had once been their hunting-grounds covered with

thriving villages, feared that they would be driven out altogether from the land of their fathers. So they prepared to defend themselves; and, when a friendly Indian revealed their plans to the people of Plymouth, they murdered him. Three of the Wampanoags were tried for this crime by the Puritans, found guilty, and hanged.

3. Philip knew the power of the English, and had tried to avoid war; but he could now restrain his followers no longer. Dividing into parties of twenty or thirty, they fell upon the frontier villages and farm-houses of Massachusetts, burned them to the ground, killed their occupants, and were off to the forest before any aid could arrive. Lying in ambush for the parties sent out against them, they cut off the flower of the settlements, and spread terror everywhere.

4. A few days after the war commenced, Captain Church with thirty-six men was attacked on the sea-shore by three hundred Indians. They took their posts behind some rocks, and defended themselves for six hours. At last, as night was setting in, their ammunition gave out. It would have fared badly with the bold Puritans, if a sloop had not just at this time come up and taken them off. Captain Church escaped, though a bullet passed through his hair.

5. Meanwhile Philip, who threw himself into the war with all his powers, had gone among the neighboring tribes, and persuaded them to join him. In a few months he found himself at the head of three thousand men. With these, when cold weather set in, he repaired to a large swamp in the country of his allies, the Narragansetts, and, building a fort, prepared to winter there. Now was the time for the English. A thousand men were sent in December against King Philip. They found the Indian fort on an island in

the swamp. The only way to reach it was by crossing a tree which at one point had been thrown across the deep stagnant water.

6. Several times the English tried to get across, but were driven back with loss. At last they succeeded in entering the fort. It

Puritans attacking King Philip's Fort.

contained five hundred wigwams, which were soon in flames. The Indians, though they fought bravely, were totally defeated. Numbers of them were killed; but Philip and Ca-non'-chet, the Narragansett chief, got away in safety. Hard indeed was the lot of those who escaped. Without shelter and almost without food, they were exposed to the fierce storms of a severe winter.

7. Three or four months after "the Swamp Fight", Canonchet was captured. Still he was as proud as ever. When a young soldier asked him some questions, he replied, "Child, you do not understand war. Let your chief come; I will answer him." They

FALL OF KING PHILIP.

offered him his life, if he would persuade the Indians to make peace; but he refused with scorn. He was then sentenced to be shot.

8. Philip, meanwhile, rested not, burning towns, and torturing his prisoners. His men, however, suffered much from hunger, sometimes having nothing to eat but the clams on the sea-shore, which they had to go miles to obtain. Many of them now fell off, and others were killed or captured by Captain Church, who had taken the field. Among those taken were the wife and son of Philip. This broke Philip's heart. Deserted by all but a few faithful followers, hunted down by the English, he could only die like an Indian warrior.

9. With his few remaining men, Philip now took refuge in a swamp near the head of Narragansett Bay. Here Captain Church surrounded him. A party of English, penetrating the swamp, reached the Indian camp at sunrise. In trying to escape, Philip approached a tree behind which an Englishman and an Indian deserter were stationed. The Englishman aimed at him, but the dew had wet his powder, and his gun missed fire. The Indian deserter then shot his former chief through the heart.

10. Thus perished this great chief, and with his fall the war ceased. Six hundred of the best men of New England had been slain; six hundred houses had been burned by the savages. The Indians had suffered still more. Two whole tribes were destroyed. For some years after this, New England enjoyed peace.

QUESTIONS.—1. What war broke out in 1675? Who was Philip? Of what tribe was he chief? Where did the Wampanoags live? Where did the Narragansetts live?—2. What was the cause of King Philip's war?—3. How was the war commenced by the savages?—4. Give an account of Captain Church's encounter with the Indians.—5. In a few months, how many men did King Philip raise? Where did he get them? What did he do when cold weather set in? What measures were now taken by the English? What was the only way of reaching Philip's fort?—6. Describe the swamp fight. How did it result? Who got away in safety? What was the lot of those who escaped?—7. What became of Canonchet? How did he answer a young soldier who asked him some questions?—8. Meanwhile, what was Philip engaged in doing? From what did his men suffer? What became of many of them? What broke Philip's heart? What now alone was left him?—9. Where did Philip at last take refuge? By whom was he surrounded? Give an account of Philip's death.—10. What did King Philip's war cost New England? What were its consequences to the Indians? After this, what was the state of things in New England?

LESSON XVIII.

VIRGINIA.—INDIAN TROUBLES.—BACON'S REBELLION.

1. We must now return to Virginia. When Powhatan died, his brother succeeded him. He soon became an enemy to the English,—and not without reason; for some of the settlers treated the Indians very ill, driving them from their own wigwams and robbing them of their corn. The Indians resolved on vengeance. They pretended to be fonder than ever of the English, and brought them presents of game. But all at once, on an appointed day, they fell on every settlement in the colony with war-whoop and tomahawk.

2. The night before, a friendly Indian had disclosed the plot to the people of Jamestown, and here the savages were driven back; but everywhere else they were successful. The settlers were taken off their guard; their houses and barns were burned. A bloody war thus arose. No one could till the fields. Food became scarce; and, though the Indians were at last put down, it was long before the colony recovered from the effects of the massacre.

3. In 1644, the same crafty chief, the brother of Powhatan, got up another plot among his people for murdering the Virginians. He was now over a hundred years old, but as cunning as ever. He laid his plans so well that the settlers were surprised, and several

hundred killed. A party, however, was sent out against the Indians, and the old chief himself was captured. He was brought a prisoner to Jamestown, and there cruelly shot by the sentinel who was guarding him.

4. At this time, Berkeley was governor of Virginia. At first he was much liked; but, when the people found that he kept them down and taxed them to enrich himself, they turned against him. One of the chief things which they complained of was that he would not take measures to protect them from the natives. He made money by selling licenses to trade with the Indians, and was unwilling to provoke a war, for it would interfere with his profits.

5. About thirty years after the fall of Powhatan's brother, as related above, the Indians again became troublesome. Again they had been provoked by cruelty on the part of the whites. In vain the people begged Governor Berkeley to send out a force to protect the frontier. There was at this time in the colony a brave and talented young man named Bacon, who had lately come over from England. Urged by his friends, and hearing of several murders committed by the Indians on his own plantation, he raised a body of men, pursued the savages, and defeated them.

6. Bacon did this without the governor's permission, and Berkeley, choosing to regard the act as treason, raised a force and marched against him. A great part of the year 1676 was spent in a struggle between Bacon and the governor. At last Bacon obtained a decided advantage. Berkeley was driven from Jamestown; and, to prevent it from falling again into his hands, it was burned to the ground. In the engraving you see some of the patriots setting fire to their own houses.

7. In the midst of his success, Bacon died. Berkeley at once resumed the chief power. Those who had taken part in "Bacon's

Rebellion", as it was called, were persecuted without mercy. Over twenty persons were put to death. The people were oppressed

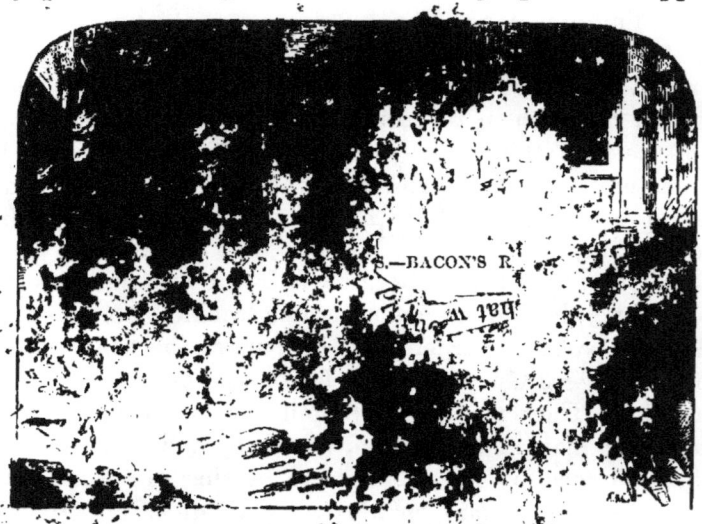

more than ever, and rejoiced when at last the tyrant sailed for England. There he was treated with the contempt he deserved, and he soon died of mortification.

8. The people of Virginia did not gain much by a change of governors. For some years they were ruled by men who tried to extort from them all they could. They struggled bravely for their rights, but for a time without success.

9. Jamestown was never rebuilt. There were, at this time, no other towns in Virginia; for the colony was divided into large plantations, on which corn and tobacco were raised. Journeys were made in boats or on horseback. The roads were mere bridle-paths through the forests. When the traveller came to a stream, he had

to swim his horse over it, for there were neither ferries nor bridges. The houses were mostly of logs, and one story high. The windows were closed with shutters, for want of glass. There were no newspapers, and few if any schools. How things have changed within two hundred years!

QUESTIONS.—1. By whom was Powhatan succeeded in Virginia? What made Powhatan's brother an enemy to the English? On what did the Indians resolve? Give an account of their plot.—2. How was Jamestown saved? What took place in the other settlements in Virginia? What followed?—3. What took place in 1644? What became of the crafty old chief?—4. Who was governor of Virginia at this time? How did the people feel towards Berkeley? Why was he unwilling to provoke a war with the natives? —5. What took place about thirty years after the fall of Powhatan's brother? Who rose up in defence of the colony? What led him to do so?—6. How did Berkeley regard this proceeding of Bacon's? What did he do? How was a great part of the year 1676 spent? How did the struggle result? What does the engraving represent?—7. What became of Bacon? What was done to those who had taken part in Bacon's rebellion? Where did Berkeley finally go? How was he treated?—8. What kind of governors did the Virginians have for some years? What struggle was carried on?—9. Was Jamestown ever rebuilt? How was the colony divided? Describe the state of things in Virginia two hundred years ago.

LESSON XIX.

CAROLINA.—PENNSYLVANIA.

1. NORTH CAROLINA.—In 1653, some planters from Virginia, invited by the fine soil and pleasant climate, moved towards the south, and settled in what is now North Carolina. Ten years afterwards, the King of England granted the country from Virginia to Florida to several of his favorites. They drew up a plan for a great empire. A few lords were to have all the power, while the people were to do the work. This did not suit the free and

hardy settlers. They insisted on their rights, and the great lords had to yield.

2. SOUTH CAROLINA.—The first settlement in South Carolina was made in 1670, by emigrants from England. In 1672, Charleston, now the largest city in the state, was founded. The country was so delightful that emigrants were attracted to it in great numbers from Scotland, Ireland, and France. The plan that had been drawn up for exalting a few lords at the expense of the people, would not answer here any more than in North Carolina, and was soon laid aside.

3. For a time the people of both North and South Carolina had some trouble with their governors. These governors, for the most part, neither knew nor cared what was for the good of the colonists, but tried to extort from them all the money they could. The people, however, would not submit. After a long struggle, they succeeded in establishing their rights. Both colonies were then happy and prosperous.

4. Rice and cotton are now among the chief productions of South Carolina. Rice came from some seed which was brought from Madagascar, an island on the coast of Africa. Cotton was raised near Jamestown, soon after it was founded; but the tobacco crop was found more profitable, and it was not till about 1700 that much attention was paid to cotton.

5. PENNSYLVANIA.—The Swedes who settled Delaware spread out towards the north, and had some thriving plantations within the limits of what is now called Pennsylvania. They were conquered by the Dutch, you remember; and the Dutch in turn yielded to the English. After remaining for a time under the government of New York, the region west of the Delaware was transferred to William Penn, and called from him Pennsylvania.

6. William Penn was a Quaker. The Quakers were a pure, good people,—but in some things peculiar. They wore broad-brimmed hats, which they would not take off before lord, or judge, or even the King himself. They called no man *Mister*. They would not address the King as *Your Majesty*, but called him *Friend Charles* or *Friend James*, as the case might be. They thought war was wrong, and wished to live in peace and love with all men.

7. The Quakers were cruelly persecuted in England. William Penn himself had been thrown into prison, and suffered much on account of his opinions. He thought it would be a great thing to establish a colony where the Quakers could be free and happy. Now, the King had owed his father, who was a famous admiral, a

Penn's Treaty with the Indians.

large sum of money; and Penn, in payment of the debt, obtained a grant of land in the new world, as mentioned above.

8. Penn, with a large company of Quakers, reached the shore of America in 1682. The next year, he laid out on the Delaware the fine city of Philadelphia, now the second in size in the Union. Penn treated all men honestly. He bought his land of the Swedes and Indians. Calling the Indians together under a great elm, he made them presents, assured them of his love, and asked their friendship in return. The Red Men met him kindly. They promised to live in peace with him and his children as long as sun and moon should endure.

9. The Indians kept their word. For seventy years, Pennsylvania had no trouble with the natives. The people enjoyed a free government, and numbers flocked there from other parts of the new world and from Europe. In three years Philadelphia grew more than New York had done in fifty years. But Penn did not profit by its prosperity. He was unjustly deprived of his rights in the colony, and died in poverty.

QUESTIONS.—1. When and by whom was North Carolina first settled? Ten years afterwards, what grant was made? What kind of a plan was drawn up for the government of Carolina? How did the settlers like this?—2. When and by whom was South Carolina first settled? When was Charleston founded? From what countries were emigrants attracted? How did the plan drawn up for the government of Carolina succeed here?—3. What difficulties arose with the governors? How did they result?—4. What are among the chief products of South Carolina? Where did rice come from? What is said of the raising of cotton?—5. Give the early history of the first settlements in what is now Pennsylvania. To whom was this region finally transferred? Whence did it receive its name?—6. What was William Penn? Describe the Quakers.—7. How were the Quakers treated in England? How had William Penn been treated? How was it that he obtained a grant in the new world?—8. When did Penn and his Quakers reach America? What did he do the next year? How did Penn treat all men? Give an account of his treaty with the Indians.—9. How long was Pennsylvania free from troubles with the natives? What is said of the growth of Philadelphia? What became of Penn?

LESSON XX.

INDIAN MISSIONS.—FRENCH EXPLORERS.

1. The Puritans were moral and industrious, but stern and formal. They cropped their hair close to their heads, and were opposed to wigs and veils. They thought it wicked for women to wear lace, silk hoods, or flowing sleeves. They observed the Sabbath strictly, and commenced it on Saturday evening. They liked very long prayers and sermons, and punished those who stayed away from church.

2. The Puritans had fled from England to escape persecution. Yet, when they got the power in the new world, they persecuted others. The colony of Massachusetts Bay, you remember, drove out Roger Williams. They treated Quakers still worse, fining and whipping such as were found within the limits of the colony. At last, they even put several Quakers to death. How could they think that such cruelty was pleasing to God?

3. Towards the Indians the Puritans showed a better spirit. John Eliot and other good men went among them, and tried to make them Christians. Eliot translated the Bible into their language, and opened a school for Indian youth. He taught the women to spin, and the men to dig. His kindness won their hearts, and many of the natives in Eastern Massachusetts received the truths he taught.

4. The Puritans were not alone in trying to convert the Indians. We learned that the French at an early date explored the St. Law-

rence River. In 1608, they founded Quebec on its left bank. The trade in furs with the Indians was found profitable, and various French settlements were made in different parts of what is now called Canada. With the traders came out a number of Roman Catholic priests and Jesuits, who travelled far out in the north-west and preached to the Indians.

5. Several little forts were built by these French priests in what is now the states of Michigan and Illinois. It was then of course a wilderness. Torture and death were often the reward of the devoted missionaries. Even after having once suffered much and escaped, they would go back to preach to the same savages that had ill-treated them.

6. This was the case with Father Jogues [*zhōg*]. The Dutch redeemed him from the Mohawks after he had been nearly tortured to death. He found his way back to Canada; but shortly after, when a missionary was to be sent to these same Mohawks, he offered himself for the work, and went, saying, "I shall never return". His words were fulfilled. Soon after his arrival, the savages declared he had blighted their crop, and put him to death.

7. Marquette [*mar-ket'*] and Joliet [*zhole-ya'*], two devoted French missionaries, in the course of their wanderings, discovered the upper part of the Mississippi, as De Soto had the lower part more than a hundred years before. They sailed some distance down the great river.. The Indians along its banks were friendly, and feasted them with hominy and fish. Marquette afterwards undertook another expedition. He landed to say his prayers on the bank of a stream in Michigan, and died there while engaged in his devotions.

8. The greatest of these French explorers was La Salle [*lah sal'*]. He set out for the west in the first sail-boat that ever crossed Lake Ontario. He met with many adventures, built forts, traded with

the Indians, and went where white men had never been before. Part of his company discovered the Falls of Saint Anthony in the Mississippi. In 1682, he sailed down the Mississippi to the Gulf of Mexico, and called the country Louisiana, after Louis XIV., King of France.

9. La Salle then went to France, to obtain the means of founding a colony at the mouth of the Mississippi. He was intrusted with several ships, and a large amount of stores. But his storeship was wrecked on the coast of what is now called Texas. He could not find the mouth of the great river. Leaving some of his men to settle in Texas, he set out with the rest, to find his way across the continent to Canada.

10. La Salle had not gone far when he was killed by one of his company. The murderer himself soon after perished, and few of the party succeeded in reaching Canada. Though La Salle failed to plant a permanent colony, his expedition gave the French King a claim to the whole valley of the Mississippi.

QUESTIONS.—1. Describe the Puritans.—2. Why had the Puritans fled from England? How did they act when they got the power in the new world? Whom did they drive out? How did they treat Quakers?—3. What spirit did the Puritans display towards the Indians? What was done by Eliot? What success did Eliot meet with?—4. What other people sent missionaries among the Indians? What river was explored by the French? What city was founded by them in 1608? Where were various French settlements made? Who came out with the traders?—5. Where were several little forts built by the French? What reward did the missionaries often meet with? How did they show their devotion?—6. Tell the story of Father Jogues.—7. By whom was the upper part of the Mississippi discovered? Give an account of their wanderings. What afterwards happened to Marquette?—8. Who was the greatest of these French explorers? Give an account of La Salle's wanderings. What discovery was made by part of his company? What did La Salle do in 1682?—9. What did La Salle next do? What accident befell him? Where did he finally try to make his way?—10. What was the fate of La Salle? What became of his party? What claim did the French King base on La Salle's discoveries?

LESSON XXI.

KING WILLIAM'S WAR.

1. The French now possessed many posts in Canada and the far west, and had great influence with some of the native tribes. The English settlements were still more numerous, and stronger. So it is not strange that the two parties should have been jealous of each other. In 1689, troubles arose between the Kings of France and England, and hostilities at once commenced in the new world. As William III. now held the crown of England, this was called King William's War.

2. The first thing the French did was to excite their Indian allies against the English. There was an old man called Major Waldron, living in Dover, New Hampshire, who had once treated the natives cruelly, and to whom some of them were in debt for goods. About dark one night, a couple of squaws knocked at his door, and asked to stay there all night, as they were very tired. Major Waldron told them that they might; but, as soon as the family were asleep, they opened the door and let in a band of Indians.

3. They set the old man on a table. He had been a magistrate; and, mocking him, they cried out, "Judge Indians now, as you used to do." Then the cruel savages who owed him money, drew their knives across his breast, saying that thus they crossed out their accounts. After killing Major Waldron, they attacked the neighboring houses, putting to death all whom they could.

4. The following winter, a body of French and Indians surprised Sche-nec'-ta-dy. This was a flourishing village, sixteen miles from Albany. There was a wall of palisades around it, but the sentinel had gone to sleep, and the assailants entered through the gate.

The inhabitants were roused by the terrible war-whoop and the crackling flames of their houses. Some were killed in their beds. Others fled into the wilderness in their night-clothes. The rest were driven off as captives, and the town was reduced to ruins. Other places on the frontier suffered in the same way.

5. These outrages at last roused the English. They sent two expeditions against the French at Montreal and Quebec. One was beaten back, and the other returned without effecting anything. Throughout this war, which lasted eight years, the French and their Indian allies had the better of the English.

6. Mrs. Dustin showed a daring spirit. She was lying sick, with a young babe beside her, when a band of Indians fell upon the house. They killed the poor infant, and made her get up, sick as she was, and go with them. Mr. Dustin was working in a field near by. He could not help her; but, telling his children to run for the woods, he kept the Indians off with his gun, and thus with difficulty saved them.

7. Mrs. Dustin, her nurse, and a boy, were driven off many miles to the north. Threatened every day with death, they at last resolved to risk their lives in an effort to escape. The boy told his master that he wanted to make a great warrior, and asked where he should strike a person in order to kill him. The savage showed him, and he told Mrs. Dustin and the nurse. That same night, the three softly arose. They struck the sleeping Indians in the way the boy had been shown, and killed the whole party that had captured them. Then they seized on a canoe, paddled down the river, and were soon among their friends, who had given them up as lost.

QUESTIONS.—1. What cause was there for jealousy between the French and English? In 1689, what took place? What was this war called, and why?—2. What was the first step taken by the French? What stratagem was practised by the Indians in Dover,

New Hampshire?—3 How did the Indians treat Major Waldron? What did they do to the neighboring houses?—4. Give an account of the attack on Schenectady.—5. What expeditions were sent out by the English? What was their success? Which side had the better throughout King William's War?—6. Give an account of the capture of Mrs. Dustin.—7. What was done with Mrs. Dustin? How did she escape?

LESSON XXII.

QUEEN ANNE'S WAR.—THE SOUTH-WEST.—GEORGIA FOUNDED.

1. In 1702, another war broke out, between the French and Spanish and the English. It was called, from the Queen of England, Queen Anne's War. In the new world, hostilities began in the south-west. The governor of South Carolina marched against the Spaniards at Saint Augustine, Florida. Before he could take the castle, two Spanish vessels appeared off the coast, and he had to leave his stores and run away. He afterwards set out against the Indian allies of the French and Spanish, and succeeded in burning several of their villages and taking a number of prisoners.

2. The French and Spanish in return made an attack on Charleston. They were bravely met by the inhabitants, who drove them back, and took a French frigate in the harbor. Though thus successful, the planters of Carolina suffered much for several years from the incursions of the savages, who were excited against them by the French and Spanish.

3. In the winter of 1704, some French and Indians from Canada made a descent on Deerfield, in the northern part of Massachusetts. They were expected, and sentinels were posted every night. But the cunning Frenchman kept his men in the woods till daybreak, when the guard was dismissed. Then, climbing up the snow, which was piled to the top of the palisades, they were in the town in a moment.

4. Every house in Deerfield was burned but one, and that was riddled with bullets. Many were killed, and still more made prisoners. Among the latter were Mr. Williams, the minister of the place, his wife, and five children. They were driven many miles through the snow; and at last Mrs. Williams, who was sick, sank from exhaustion, and was killed before her husband's eyes. After remaining a prisoner many months, Mr. Williams was ransomed, and returned to his friends, with all his children but a daughter seven years old.

5. Years rolled on, and Deerfield was rebuilt. One day, a woman dressed like a squaw entered the town. Her face was unlike an Indian's, and the people asked her who she was. She answered that she was the lost daughter of Mr. Williams; that she was married to an Indian, and had several children in Canada. The people begged her to stay with them; but she would not leave her husband and children, and went back to Canada.

6. The King of France was not discouraged by La Salle's ill success. He sent out more emigrants, who found the mouth of the Mississippi, sailed up the river, and built a fort where Natchez now stands. In 1718, the city of New Orleans was laid out. At first it grew but slowly; but now it is the great city of the south-west.

7. The colonists of Louisiana, as this whole region was then called, soon got in trouble with the natives. The Natchez Indians had a village near the French fort, which the French wanted to seize and turn into a plantation. This roused the Natchez, who fell on the fort and put to death all except the women and children. The people of New Orleans avenged this massacre by destroying the whole tribe.

8. The last settled of the colonies was Georgia. In 1733, Oglethorpe [*o'-gel-thorp*], having obtained a grant from George II., King

of Great Britain, in whose honor he named his colony, reached the Savannah River with a company of emigrants. The beautiful city of Savannah was founded, with wide and regular streets, and large gardens around the houses. More emigrants came over, and through the wisdom of Oglethorpe the colony flourished.

9. Oglethorpe treated the Indians kindly, and they met him in the same spirit. Soon after his arrival, several chiefs came to welcome him. They brought him a buffalo skin, adorned with the head and feathers of an eagle, in token of their friendship, and asked him to love and protect their families.

10. We have now had an account of the founding of the Thirteen Colonies. See if you can remember them in order, with the date of each.

1. Virginia, by the English, at Jamestown, in 1607.
2. New York, by the Dutch, at New Amsterdam, in 1614.
3. New Jersey, by Dutch traders, at Bergen, in 1618.
4. Massachusetts, by English Puritans, at Plymouth, in 1620.
5. New Hampshire, by the English, at Dover and Portsmouth, in 1623.
6. Delaware, by the Swedes and Finns, in 1627.
7. Maryland, by the English under Lord Baltimore, in 1634.
8. Connecticut, by Puritans from Massachusetts, in 1635.
9. Rhode Island, by Roger Williams, at Providence, in 1636.
10. Pennsylvania, by Swedes from Delaware, in 1643.
  By English Quakers, at Philadelphia, in 1683.
11. North Carolina, by emigrants from Virginia, in 1653.
12. South Carolina, by the English, near Charleston, in 1670.
13. Georgia, by the English, at Savannah, in 1733.

QUESTIONS.—1. What war broke out in 1702? Where did hostilities begin in the new world? What was done by the governor of South Carolina? What expedition did he afterwards undertake?—2. What attack was made in return by the French and Spanish? What success did they meet with? From what did the planters of Carolina suffer?—3. In 1704, what place was attacked? How did the French and Indians get inside of the palisades?—4. How did the attack on Deerfield terminate? Who were taken prisoners? What became of Mrs. Williams? What became of Mr. Williams and most of his family?—5. Tell the story of Mr. Williams' little daughter.—6. What settlement was made by the French in the south-west? When was New Orleans laid out? What rank does this city now hold?—7. What led to the destruction of the French fort near Natchez? How did the people of New Orleans avenge this massacre?—8. Which of the colonies was settled last? When and by whom was Georgia settled? What city was first founded?—9. How did Oglethorpe treat the Indians? Give an account of their visit to him.—10. State, in order, by whom and when each of the Thirteen Colonies was founded.

LESSON XXIII.

WASHINGTON'S EXPEDITION.

1. As years rolled on, both French and English increased rapidly in America. No boundary line had been agreed upon between the two nations. Each was jealous of the other. The French claimed the rich valleys of the Ohio and Mississippi, on the ground of having first explored them. They sent out agents to make friends of the Indians, and broke up an English post on the frontier, carrying off the traders to Canada.

2. The Indians who lived near the Ohio became alarmed at these movements. They sent one of their warriors to the French, to say that the Great Spirit had given these lands to them. But the French commander replied, "It is my land, and I will have it." The Indians then made a treaty with the English; and the governor of Virginia determined to send a messenger to the French, to forbid their trespassing on territory which he said belonged to England.

3. The person selected for this mission was GEORGE WASHINGTON,—the great Washington, "the father of his country",—then a youth of twenty-one. Washington was born in a Virginia farm-house

near the Potomac River. He was brought up by a good mother, who taught him to love what was true and noble.

4. Once, when a new hatchet had been given him, he went around trying its edge in the garden, and thus ruined a favorite cherry-tree of his father's. When his father asked who had done the mischief, the little George was tempted to deny the act. He hesitated for a moment, but then cried, "Father, I can not tell a lie; I cut the tree." "Come to my heart, my boy," answered George's father, folding him in his arms; "I had rather lose a thousand trees than find falsehood in my son."

5. George was an excellent horseman. His mother had two favorite horses, one of which was not used to the saddle. As this horse was feeding on the lawn one day, some young men proposed to mount it. They tried in vain, however; it set them all at defiance. George, who was one of the youngest present, then made the attempt. In spite of its plunging and kicking, he succeeded in getting on its back, and kept his seat there, till, after a furious race, the animal fell exhausted.

6. At school George was the leader of all the boys in both play and study. He became a good surveyor, and soon after leaving school was employed to survey a large tract of wild land on the Potomac. He camped out in the woods, shot his own game, cooked it for himself, used a chip for his dish, and his fingers for forks. He soon became known for his courage and fidelity, and this led the governor of Virginia to choose him for his messenger to the French.

7. The French fort lay in the north-west of Pennsylvania. The route thither ran through forests and swamps, and over rivers swollen by rain and snow. It was with great difficulty Washington reached it. He delivered his message without effect. The French

1753] WASHINGTON'S EXPEDITION. 77

commander pointed to his boats, all ready for starting, and told him that in the spring he intended sailing down the Ohio, and destroying every English post he met with.

8. Several friendly Indians had accompanied Washington, and these the French tried to entice from him with rum and presents. Washington could hardly get them away. At last, finding he could do nothing, he set out on his return, having first learned all he could about the plans of the French. His journey home was full of dangers. It was extremely cold. The horses were disabled, and he had to go on foot through the snow. A treacherous Indian guide fired at his head at the distance of a few feet, but missed his aim.

9. At length, with a single companion, he came to a deep river, full of drifting ice. Having made a raft, they got on board, and

tried to push it across with poles. It soon became jammed between cakes of ice. Washington, while trying to steady the raft with his pole, was jerked into the water, and narrowly escaped drowning. In the engraving you see him struggling amid the ice.

10. Through all the dangers of the way, Washington was preserved by a Higher Power. He made his report to the governor of Virginia, and was praised by all for the gallantry with which he had discharged his duty. A long war between the French and English followed, which is known as the French and Indian War.

QUESTIONS.—1. What difficulty again arose between the French and the English? What was the ground of the French claim? What steps were taken by the French?—2. What passed between the Indians living near the Ohio and the French? With whom did the Indians then make a treaty? What was done by the governor of Virginia?—3. Who was selected for this mission? How old was Washington then? Where was he born? By whom was he brought up?—4. What story is told, showing Washington's love of truth in boyhood?—5. Relate the story about George's skill in horsemanship.—6. What position did George take in school? How was he employed after leaving school? What led the governor of Virginia to choose him for his messenger?—7. Where did the French fort lie? What is said of the route thither? What effect did Washington's message produce?—8. By whom had Washington been accompanied? What did the French try to do with these Indians? At last, what was Washington obliged to do? What is said of the journey home?—9. Give an account of Washington's narrow escape amid the drifting ice.—10. On making his report, for what was Washington commended? What war followed?

LESSON XXIV.

FRENCH AND INDIAN WAR.—BRADDOCK'S DEFEAT.

1. By Washington's advice, the English commenced a fort where Pittsburg, in Pennsylvania, now stands. Before its completion it was captured by the French, who finished it and called it Fort Du Quesne [*dukane*].

2. A force commanded by Washington had been sent out to

BRADDOCK'S EXPEDITION.

garrison this post. Though too late to save it, they surprised a body of French by a night attack, and completely defeated them. Washington was soon after surrounded in a stockade which he had constructed, by a large force of French and Indians. He had to surrender, but was allowed to retain his stores, and march out with the honors of war.

3. In 1755, General Braddock came over from Great Britain with a powerful army, to attack the French. He advanced against Fort Du Quesne, moving but slowly, in consequence of having to make his own road through the wilderness. Washington joined his army, and warned the general to be on his guard against Indian ambuscades. But Braddock paid no attention to his warnings. The savages, he said, could do no harm to British troops.

4. When Braddock's army was within a few miles of Fort Du Quesne, a deadly fire was suddenly poured in upon them; and Indian yells rent the air in front and on each side. The savages were concealed behind trees and rocks, and the British were cut down without a chance of returning their fire. The van was seized with a panic, and fell back on the main body. The Virginia Rangers, who were used to Indian warfare, stood their ground bravely for a time; but the rest were thrown into confusion, left their baggage, and fled from the field.

5. Braddock was mortally wounded while trying to rally his men. The chief command then fell to Washington. He threw himself into the thickest of the fight. Two horses were shot under him. Four balls passed through his coat. The Indians aimed at him again and again; still he escaped uninjured. But in vain he strove to turn the fortunes of the day.

6. The British fled many miles, destroying their artillery and stores. The fine army of Braddock was broken up, and that by a

much smaller force of French and Indians. The French commander had at first thought of abandoning the fort. One of his officers persuaded him to stay and meet the enemy; and, with the aid of his Indian allies, he was, as we have seen, completely successful.

7. The English colonists had expected much from Braddock, and were greatly disappointed at his defeat. In the north, however, they had better success. Near Lake George, in the state of New York, they defeated a large army of French and Indians, who were making a descent on one of their forts. They also conquered a large tract lying east of Maine, now called New Brunswick.

8. In 1756, the French sent over a distinguished general named Montcalm, to command their forces in America. Taking advantage of the inactivity of the English general, Montcalm captured a number of places. In 1757, marching down from Canada into the state of New York with a large force of French and Indians, he laid siege to Fort William Henry, on the southern shore of Lake George. This post was bravely defended by its commander, who hoped for relief from a British army under General Webb, at another fort, only fourteen miles off.

9. But Webb was afraid to meet Montcalm, and let the garrison of Fort William Henry take care of itself. Still the officer in command gallantly held out. It was not till half his cannon burst, and his ammunition gave out, that he agreed to surrender. Honorable terms were granted. The troops were to be allowed to join their comrades at the other fort.

10. No sooner, however, had they commenced marching out of Fort William Henry, than the savages in Montcalm's army began to rob and murder them. A general massacre ensued. In spite of the efforts of the French officers, only a part of the British army

escaped. Up to this time the French had been generally successful. They now possessed twenty times as much territory in America as the English.

QUESTIONS.—1. Where did Washington advise the erection of a fort? What became of this fort? What did the French call it?—2. What victory was soon after achieved by Washington? What then befell him?—3. Who came over in 1755? What post did Braddock proceed to attack? Who joined his army? What advice did Washington give Braddock? What reply did Braddock make?—4. Give an account of the surprise of Braddock's army. How did the Virginia Rangers behave? What is said of the rest of the army?—5. What befell Braddock? Who then took the command? What dangers did Washington escape?—6. What became of Braddock's fine army? What had the French commander at first intended? What made him change his mind?—7. What success did the English colonists have in the north? What large tract did they conquer?—8. In 1756, what French general came over? What did Montcalm do in 1757? On whom did the commander of Fort William Henry rely for aid?—9. Why did not Webb go to relieve the fort? How long did he hold out? On what terms did he surrender?—10. Give an account of the massacre that followed the surrender. Up to this time, which party had generally been successful? How did the French territory in America now compare with the English?

LESSON XXV.

CLOSE OF THE FRENCH AND INDIAN WAR.

1. The English losses had been caused by the inefficiency of their generals. In 1758, therefore, *** selected better leaders. Several expeditions were planned. C*** e resulted in the capture of Louisburg, a strong French p*** an island north-east of Nova Scotia. The French com*** held out till his ships were taken, his cannon destroyed, and *** works battered down. Nor would he have surrendered then, had it not been for the prayers of the inhabitants.

2. Montcalm, the gallant French general, was at Ticonderoga.

Here he was attacked by a superior force of English, but he drove them back with loss. An English expedition directed against Fort Du Quesne was more successful. One division of the army, sent out to reconnoitre, was defeated; but, when Washington and his brave Virginians approached the fort, the French commander blew up the magazine, set fire to the works, and retreated with his men in boats.

3. Washington raised his country's flag over the ruins. A new block-house, represented in the cut, was erected. The place was called Pittsburg, after Pitt, an eminent English statesman. Returning soon after to Virginia, Washington was received with great honor. The district in which he lived had elected him to the House of Burgesses, as the legislature of the colony was called. When he took his seat in that body, the Speaker rose and thanked him in the name of his coun-

try for his distinguished services. Washington rose to reply—blushed—stammered—trembled—but could not say a word. "Sit down, Mr. Washington," said the Speaker; "your modesty equals your courage, and that surpasses the power of any language I possess."

4. The strongest place now in possession of the French was Quebec. This had been founded about the same time as James-

town. The fort stood on an almost perpendicular bluff, two hundred feet high. It was strongly built, and defended by a large army under Montcalm. This post the English determined to take. The heroic Wolfe, with eight thousand men, was sent against it. They arrived in the summer of 1759.

5. For several months Wolfe lay before Quebec. He made various attempts, but was baffled in all by the strength of the place. He could see but one chance of success, and that, slight as it was, he resolved to try. While sailing up the river, he had espied, a short distance above the fort, a steep rough path running up the face of the cliff amid rocks and bushes. This led, he was told, to the Plains of Abraham, which extended to the upper town. His plan was to land in the night, lead his men up the narrow path, surprise the French guard on the top, and then advance upon the fort.

6. This plan was carried out. In the engraving on the next page, you see Wolfe's men climbing up the cliff. Supporting themselves by roots and bushes, they reached the top, and put to flight the French guard which had fired on them as they approached the summit. By dawn the whole English army was on the heights. Montcalm was thunderstruck when he received these tidings. His men were at once in motion. A bloody battle took place. The English were successful. Wolfe fell at the moment of victory, thanking God for his success, and declaring that he died happy.

7. Montcalm, also, was mortally wounded, while trying to rally his men. He had done all he could to save the day, but in vain. The French fled into the town, and three days afterwards Quebec surrendered to the English. The next year Montreal was taken, and with it all Canada fell into the hands of the English. It has ever since remained in their possession.

8. Thus ended the French and Indian War. It lasted over six years, and cost the lives of thousands of brave men. Wolfe and

Wolfe's Army ascending to the Plains of Abraham.—The fort, or citadel, of Quebec is on the top of the bluff at the right of the engraving. At its base, is what is called the Lower Town. The bay in which the boats landed, is known as Wolfe's Cove.

Montcalm, the two gallant generals, were much lamented. The English have since raised a monument, bearing the name of each, on the spot where the battle was fought. Though England spent a great deal of money in this struggle, she in return vastly increased her possessions in the new world.

QUESTIONS.—1. By what had the English losses been caused? What did they therefore do? What French post was captured? How long did the commander hold out?— 2. What other post was attacked? With what result? Give an account of the English attack on Fort Du Quesne.—3. What was erected on the site of Fort Du Quesne? To what was the name changed? How was Washington received, on his return to Virginia? What passed in the House of Burgesses?—4. What was the strongest place now in possession of the French? How was Quebec situated? By whom was it defended? Who was sent against it? When?—5. How did Wolfe spend several months? What desperate plan did he at last form?—6. Give an account of the ascent. What did Montcalm do, on hearing the news? What was the result of the battle? What was Wolfe's fate?—7. What happened to Montcalm? Three days after the battle, what took place? What fell into the hands of the English, the next year?—8. How long did the French and Indian War last? How have the English honored the memory of Wolfe and Montcalm? What did England lose, and what did she gain, in this struggle?

LESSON XXVI.

TROUBLES WITH THE GOVERNORS.

1. Peace now prevailed, and the colonies would have flourished if they had been left to themselves. But the King and Parliament of England wanted to control them and interfere with their affairs. Many of the governors, for years back, had been men who cared little for the colonies. Their chief aim was to enrich themselves, and deprive the people of their rights.

2. But the hardy settlers of America were not disposed to submit. On one occasion, Andros, who had been made governor of all New England, went to Connecticut, and told the people they must give up their charter. This was a paper setting forth their rights. It had been granted to them by a previous King; but the tyrannical James II. had revoked it, and sent Andros to take it away. The people were opposed to its surrender, and crowded into the hall where the Assembly were discussing the question.

3. The charter lay open on a table. On a sudden the candles were put out, and when they were relighted the charter could not be found. A patriot had made off with it, and hidden it in the hollow of a large oak, called from this "the charter oak". Two years afterwards, the people heard that King James had been driven from his throne in England, on account of his tyranny. On this they seized Andros, sent him over to England, and drew the much-prized charter, uninjured, out of its hiding-place.

4. A few years after this, the King gave Governor Fletcher authority to command the militia of Connecticut; and he ordered them to turn out at Hartford on a certain day, for review. The people preferred having their own officers command them. When Fletcher arrived, he found a large body of men assembled, with their captain, named Wadsworth, at their head. "Read the King's order, by which I am to command the Connecticut militia," said Fletcher to his secretary. Just then Wadsworth gave a signal, and the drummers commenced beating their drums so loudly that the secretary could not be heard.

5. "Silence!" roared Fletcher, and beckoned to his secretary to go on. Before he could do so, the drums commenced again, drowning every other sound. "Silence!" again cried Fletcher, almost bursting with rage. The drummers stopped; but Wadsworth, stepping up fiercely with his drawn sword, bade them go on. "If you interrupt them again," said he to Fletcher, "I will make daylight shine through you." When Fletcher heard this, he concluded to leave the Connecticut militia to their own officers.

6. The French and Indian War afforded a new pretext for wringing money out of America. The King and Parliament took the ground that, as the war had been in defence of the colonies, the colonies should pay for it. So they laid duties on various articles

imported into America. The colonies were willing to bear the expense of the war. But they claimed that Parliament had no right to tax them, because they were not represented by any delegates in that body. Taxation without representation they would not submit to.

7. In 1760, Parliament took new measures for collecting the odious duty. The colonies were at once thrown into great excitement. Meetings were held, and the people protested against Parliament's assuming such despotic powers. The excitement was increased in 1765, by Parliament's passing the famous Stamp Act. By this act, all newspapers and almanacs, all bonds, notes, contracts, &c., were required to bear stamps, which were to be bought from the government at prices ranging from one cent to nearly thirty dollars. This tax the colonies determined to resist, if necessary, by force of arms.

QUESTIONS.—1. What now prevented the colonies from flourishing? What was the character of many of the governors?—2. How did the colonists feel towards their oppressive governors? What difficulty arose with Governor Andros?—3. How was the charter saved? What afterwards happened to Andros?—4, 5. What difficulty arose with Governor Fletcher? Tell what passed between him and Captain Wadsworth.—6. What afforded a new pretext for wringing money out of America? What did the King and Parliament claim? What ground was taken by the colonies?—7. What did Parliament do in 1760? What was the effect of this in the colonies? What increased the excitement? What was required by the Stamp Act? How did the colonists feel respecting this tax?

LESSON XXVII.

CAUSES OF THE REVOLUTION.

1. When the news that the Stamp Act had passed reached Virginia, the House of Burgesses was in session. Among the members

was a young lawyer of burning eloquence and fearless spirit, named Patrick Henry. Indignant at this outrage on his country's rights, he poured forth an impassioned speech, which carried all before it. So boldly did he express himself, that the cry of "Treason! Treason!" was raised in different parts of the house, by members who favored the royal cause. But nothing could withstand the torrent of Patrick Henry's eloquence. It awakened a spirit of resistance in every noble breast.

2. The people did not confine themselves to words. They burned images of those who were appointed to sell the stamps. When vessels with stamps arrived, they tolled the bells, and walked the streets dressed in mourning. They destroyed whole boxes of stamps, and threatened all who should distribute or use them. So Parliament had to repeal this act. But it still claimed the right of taxation, and laid a duty on all tea, glass, paper, and painter's colors, imported into the colonies.

3. The colonists were still dissatisfied; and, when they heard that English soldiers had been ordered to Boston, to make them submit, they were more angry than ever. The soldiers, on their arrival, treated the people insolently, while their officers screened them from punishment. They soon had a collision with the citizens of Boston, in which three of the latter were killed. This was called "the Boston Massacre".

4. Parliament at last saw fit to take off the duties from every article but tea. The colonists then determined not to use any tea. When ships containing this article came over, they would not let them land, but sent them back to England. At Boston, three ships full of tea having arrived, the governor insisted that they should not go back, but that their cargoes should be landed. So, after dark one night, a party of men disguised as Indians went on board

of the ships, and threw the tea overboard into the harbor. This was done amid the cheers of a great crowd assembled on the wharf.

Throwing over the Tea in Boston Harbor.

5. On their return, they passed a house where the British Admiral was spending the evening. Putting his head out of the window, he cried, "Well, boys, you've had a fine night for your Indian caper; but mind, you've got to pay the fiddler." "Oh! never mind," said one of the crowd; "just you come out here, and we'll settle the bill in two minutes." But the Admiral declined the invitation.

6. General Gage was now governor of Massachusetts. Instead of making friends of the people, he let his soldiers provoke them

more and more. Even the boys did not escape. The red-coats interfered with their sports, broke through their skating-ponds, and, when they complained, called them young rebels. At last they assembled in a body and went to General Gage. They boldly told

The Boston Boys and General Gage.

him how his soldiers had ill-treated them, and that they would bear it no longer. The general could not help admiring them. "Go, my brave boys," he replied, "and be assured that if my troops trouble you again they shall be punished."

7. Parliament persisted in its claims; the colonies denied them. Neither would yield. In vain General Gage tried to bribe the leading patriots. The King had not money enough to buy them. Delegates from the different colonies met at Philadelphia in 1774, to agree upon measures of resistance. Bodies of militia were formed. Officers were appointed. "Minute-men," as they were called,

agreed to shoulder their muskets at a moment's notice. Patrick Henry again raised his voice in Virginia. His thrilling words, "*Give me liberty or give me death,*" were reëchoed far and wide throughout the colonies.

QUESTIONS.—1. What took place in the House of Burgesses of Virginia, when the passage of the Stamp Act was announced? What was the effect of Patrick Henry's eloquence?—2. What acts followed on the part of the colonists? What was Parliament obliged to do? On what did it lay a duty?—3. What increased the dissatisfaction of the colonists? How did the soldiers behave on their arrival? What is meant by "the Boston massacre"?—4. What concessions did Parliament finally make? Was this sufficient? What resolution did the colonists form? Give an account of the riot at Boston.—5. What passed between the tea rioters and the British Admiral?—6. Who was now governor of Massachusetts? What course did he pursue? How were the Boston boys troubled? Give an account of their interview with General Gage.—7. What did General Gage try to do? With what success? What meeting was held in 1774? What measures were adopted? What famous words of Patrick Henry's were reëchoed throughout the colonies?

LESSON XXVIII.

COMMENCEMENT OF THE REVOLUTION.

1. In 1775, the war, long foreseen, broke out. It is known as the Revolutionary War. Early in that year, the British Parliament declared that Massachusetts was in rebellion, and sent out more troops. General Gage had already fortified Boston Neck, which connects the city with the main land. The patriots had some trouble in getting their ammunition out of Boston. They hid their cannon in loads of manure, and their powder and cartridges in market-baskets and candle-boxes. Thus they passed the sentinels unsuspected.

2. The patriots collected most of their stores at Concord, a few miles from Boston. Hearing of this, General Gage one night sent a force of eight hundred men to destroy them. It was done very

secretly; yet the patriots found out what was going on. The British, as they advanced towards Concord, heard bells ringing and guns firing in the surrounding country. These were signals for the minute-men to assemble.

3. A little more than half way between Boston and Concord was the village of Lexington. Here the British arrived shortly after daylight. They found a body of minute-men on the green. "Disperse, ye rebels!" said the British leader, riding up to them and discharging his pistol. His men then fired. Several of the Americans fell. The rest gave way. This was the first blood shed in the Revolution.

4. The British went on to Concord. Here some of them held the

bridge, while the rest went to destroy the stores. Meanwhile some

American militia-men came up, and a skirmish took place at the bridge, which you see represented in the engraving. Several fell on both sides; and, as soon as their companions came back, the British were glad to commence their homeward march. They had destroyed two cannon, had thrown a great number of cannon-balls into the river and wells, and had broken to pieces about sixty barrels of flour. Most of the stores had been carried off to a place of safety before they arrived.

5. A large quantity of flour was saved by a miller named Wheeler. It was stored in his barn, along with some of his own. When the soldiers came to search the place, Wheeler told them that he was a miller, and made his living by grinding grain. Then putting his hand on a barrel which belonged to himself, he said: "This is my flour; surely you will not destroy private property." The soldiers thought from what he said that it was all his, and went away without doing any injury.

6. The British suffered sorely on their return. The alarm had spread, and the brave men of the surrounding country came up from all sides. Posting themselves behind barns and houses, trees and fences, they poured in a deadly fire on the retreating British. In vain the latter tried to return it. All the way to Boston, they were thus harassed. Their ranks kept thinning, and they were ready to sink with fatigue. They would never have reached the city, had not fresh troops been sent to their aid.

7. The news of the battle of Lexington was the signal for a general rising. The farmer left his plough, and the mechanic his workshop. Even old men and boys hastened to arm themselves. The wife girded the sword about her husband. The mother blessed her son, and bade him go strike a blow for his country. There was many a scene like that which you see in the engraving.

8. One mother fitted out her eldest son with a fowling-piece and slugs made out of her pewter spoons. Her younger boy was only

sixteen. For him she had nothing but an old rusty sword. Giving him this, she dashed away a tear, and bade him follow his brother. "Beg or borrow a sword, my child," she said; "or you will find one. Some coward, I dare say, will be running away. Then take his gun and march forward."

9. At Barn'-sta-ble, the only child of a farmer joined a company that was about to march to Cambridge. As they passed the father's house on leaving the village, he came forth and said: "God be with you all, my friends! and, John, if you, my son, are called into battle, take care that you behave manfully, or else let me never see your face again." This was the spirit everywhere. Twenty thousand patriots were soon in arms around Boston.

THE GREEN MOUNTAIN BOYS.

QUESTIONS.—1. When did the war break out? What was it called? What was done by the British Parliament in 1775? What had General Gage already done? How did the patriots get their cannon and ammunition out of Boston?—2. Where did the patriots collect most of their stores? What movement was made by General Gage? What did the British hear, as they advanced towards Concord?—3. What place did the British reach soon after daylight? What took place at Lexington?—4. Where did the British then go? Give an account of the skirmish at Concord Bridge. What did the British destroy? What had been done with most of the stores?—5. How did Mr. Wheeler save a large quantity of flour?—6. Describe the retreat of the British to Boston. What alone enabled them to reach the city?—7. What effect did the news of the battle of Lexington produce? Describe the scene represented in the engraving.—8. What story is told of a mother and her two sons?—9. Relate the incident at Barnstable.

LESSON XXIX.

CAPTURE OF TICONDEROGA.—ETHAN ALLEN.

1. The spirit of resistance was not confined to New England. In Virginia, the governor thought it prudent to take refuge on a British vessel. The governors of North and South Carolina were also obliged to flee. Just a month after the battle of Lexington, a meeting was held at Charlotte, North Carolina. The people there went so far as to declare themselves independent of the King, and said they would maintain their freedom with their lives. This was the first Declaration of Independence.

2. Ticonderoga, an important fort on Lake Champlain, was garrisoned by British soldiers. Ethan Allen and his brave Green Mountain Boys resolved to capture this post. The Green Mountains are in Vermont; and the hardy pioneers of this region called themselves Green Mountain Boys. They assembled on the shore of the lake, opposite Ticonderoga, without the garrison's suspecting that any foe was near.

3. One of the party went to the fort, pretending to be an awk-

ward country boy, who wanted to be shaved. After learning all he could about the place, he returned to his companions. In the night they commenced crossing, but there were not boats enough to carry all the men over. As daylight approached, Allen, not daring to wait for any more, led his men up to the fort. As he drew near, a sentinel snapped his gun at the party; but it missed fire. He then ran into the fort to raise an alarm, closely followed by the Americans.

4. The frightened soldiers leaped from their beds, but it was only to find themselves prisoners. The commanding officer rushed to the door of his quarters in his night-clothes, followed by his wife. Allen, pointing to his men, bade him surrender. "By what authority," he asked, "do you command it?" "In the name of the great Jehovah and the Continental Congress," was Allen's reply. There was no help for it. The fort was surrendered, with its stores, powder, and cannon—all of which were much needed by the patriots.

5. Ethan Allen soon after planned an invasion of Canada. Trying to take Montreal, he was himself taken by the British. They put him in irons, and sent him over to England. Here he was in danger of being hanged as a rebel. It was more than two years before he was released. Sent from place to place as a prisoner, he was half starved, and treated with insult and cruelty.

6. On one British ship he was treated with kindness, and well did he repay it. There were a number of American prisoners on board, and some of them formed a plan to kill the captain and seize on the ship and a large sum of money which it contained. Having won over a number of the crew, they tried to get Allen to join them. But he indignantly refused, and told them he would peril his life in defence of the captain who had treated them all so well. Owing to his threats and persuasions, they gave up the plan.

7. Ethan Allen was as honest as he was brave. He once gave his note for one hundred and fifty dollars to a person whom he owed. When it became due, he could not pay it. He was sued, and employed a lawyer to get the matter put off till he could raise the money. He was utterly surprised when his lawyer rose in court and denied the signature of the note. Rushing up to him, he cried: "Sir, I didn't hire you to come here and lie. That's a true note. I signed it, and I'll pay it. I want no shuffling. All I want is time." He obtained the time he wanted, and the note was paid..

8. The very day on which Ethan Allen took Ticonderoga (May 10th, 1775), the Continental Congress met the second time at Philadelphia. They prepared for war in earnest. A large amount of paper money was issued. George Washington, of whom we heard before in the French and Indian War, was elected commander-in-chief. He hastened to Cambridge, near Boston, to take command of the patriots there assembled. Before he arrived, however, a large number of fresh troops from England had reached Boston, and an important battle had been fought.

QUESTIONS.—1. Where, besides in New England, was the spirit of resistance shown? What took place in Charlotte, North Carolina?—2. Where was Ticonderoga situated? Who resolved to capture it? Why were Ethan Allen's party called Green Mountain Boys? Where did they assemble?—3. How did they obtain information about the fort? Give an account of the crossing. What took place as they approached the fort?—4. What did the soldiers find, when they leaped from their beds? What passed between Allen and the commander? What was the result?—5. What did Ethan Allen soon after plan? What success did he meet with? What did the British do with him? How was he treated?—6. Tell how he once repaid the kindness of a British captain.—7. Relate an anecdote showing Allen's honesty.—8. What took place the same day on which Ticonderoga was captured? What preparations were made by Congress? Who was elected commander-in-chief? To what place did Washington hasten? What took place before Washington reached Cambridge?

LESSON XXX.

BATTLE OF BUNKER HILL.

1. In June, 1775, (before Washington had taken the chief command) ten thousand British troops lay in Boston. Nearly twice as many Americans had gathered around the city. But they were poorly armed, and many of them had never been in battle. Hearing that the British intended fortifying Bunker Hill, the American general determined to be beforehand with him. Accordingly, that same evening, he sent Colonel Prescott, with one thousand men, to take possession of Bunker Hill, and throw up a breastwork of earth for its defence.

2. The men worked silently with their pick-axes and spades all night. They heard the British sentinels at Boston cry "All's well!" But the British did not hear them, and the next morning were amazed to see a strong intrenchment commanding the city. A battle was resolved on. The flower of the British army was sent to dislodge the Americans, and the British ships in the harbor opened a fire on the hill. The roofs and steeples of Boston and the country around were filled with anxious spectators.

3. Twice the British troops charged up the hill. The Americans had been ordered to wait till they saw the whites of the enemies' eyes, and then to fire low and not waste their powder. They obeyed the order, and twice the British veterans recoiled before them. Fresh troops were then brought up, and a third attack was made. Unfortunately, the powder of the Americans now gave out. They received the British with stones and clubbed muskets. But it was useless to resist, and a retreat was ordered.

4. As they were leaving the works, General Warren, a distin-

guished patriot, fell mortally wounded. Prescott had offered him the command in the morning. He declined it, saying he had come to learn, and served in the ranks as a private. The British general rejoiced at his fall, saying it was worth that of five hundred ordinary soldiers.

5. Though driven from their ground, the Americans had greatly the advantage at Bunker Hill. They lost less than half as many men as the British, and, if their ammunition had lasted, would doubtless have remained masters of the field. A splendid monument has since been raised near the spot where Warren fell, to commemorate this battle.

6. Among those who did good service at Bunker Hill was Gen. Putnam. He was ploughing when he heard of the battle of Lexington. Leaving his plough in the field,

Bunker Hill Monument.

without even waiting to change his clothes, he mounted his horse and galloped off for Cambridge. He had served in the French and Indian War, and was nearly sixty years old; but he was strong and brave as ever.

7. Putnam's farm was in Connecticut. Here, when a young man, he was much troubled by a cunning wolf that prowled about the country, destroying what she could, and always escaping the hunters. In one night she killed seventy of his sheep and goats. Putnam and several of his neighbors resolved to hunt her to the death. They tracked her to her den, which was a deep cavern, and tried to drive her out by throwing in burning straw and sulphur; but in vain. The dogs were then sent in. They soon came out howling and badly wounded, and refused to return.

8. At last, Putnam threw off his coat, tied a rope to one of his legs, and with a torch in one hand and his loaded gun in the other, descended into the den. His companions, who were anxiously listening above, soon heard an angry growl and the sharp crack of a musket. They drew Putnam up. Again he descended, and this time, on being drawn up, he had the dead wolf by the ears.

9. Many a thrilling scene had "old Put", as his friends called him, passed through. He once, at the risk of his life, and not without some dreadful burns, saved Fort Edward from being consumed, and the magazine from exploding. At another time, he was captured by a party of Indians, who prepared to torture him. They tied him to a tree, piled up fagots around him, and set them on fire. A thunder-shower put out the flames. Again they lighted the pile. Hope had died in Putnam's bosom, when a French officer burst through the bushes, hurled the savages right and left, scattered the blazing wood, and released the prisoner.

10. Shortly before the Revolution, General Gage, in Putnam's

presence, expressed the opinion that five thousand British veterans could march from one end of America to the other unharmed. "So they might," replied Putnam, "if they behaved themselves properly, and paid for what they wanted. But should they attempt it as enemies, the American women would knock them on the head with their ladles."

QUESTIONS.—1. In June, 1775, how many British troops lay in Boston? How many Americans had gathered around the city? What movement was contemplated by the British? In view of this, what was done by the American general?—2. What was accomplished by the Americans during the night? What did the British see in the morning? What measures were taken by the British?—3. Give an account of the battle of Bunker Hill.—4. Who was killed, as the Americans were leaving the works? What had passed between Warren and Colonel Prescott? How did the British general feel, when he heard of Warren's fall?—5. Which party had the advantage in the battle of Bunker Hill? What monument has since been raised?—6. Who did good service at Bunker Hill? How was Putnam employed when he heard of the battle of Lexington? What did he do? In what war had he served? How old was he at this time?—7, 8. Tell the story of Putnam and the wolf.—9. What did Putnam once do at the risk of his life? Give an account of his rescue from the Indians by a French officer.—10. What anecdote is related of Putnam and General Gage?

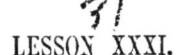

LESSON XXXI.

INVASION OF CANADA.—SIEGE OF BOSTON.

1. Ethan Allen had failed to take Montreal. This did not prevent Congress from carrying on the invasion of Canada. They hoped the Canadians would join in the Revolution. Besides, they wanted to secure a large amount of stores deposited at Quebec. General Montgomery was placed at the head of the invading force. Before long, St. John's and Montreal, two important posts, had surrendered. Quebec remained. But the American soldiers had enlisted for a certain time; this time was up. Most of them in-

sisted on returning, and Montgomery was left with but a small part of his force.

2. Just at this time, Benedict Arnold was leading a body of Americans to join their countrymen in Canada. They were pushing their way through the northern part of Maine, a pathless wilderness, and came near perishing from cold, sickness, and hunger. On one occasion, they had eaten their last ox, their last dog, and had nothing but roots and their moose-skin moccasins to live on, when they were relieved by the arrival of timely supplies.

3. Joined by this heroic band, Montgomery lost no time in laying siege to Quebec. But his few small cannon could make no impression on its strong walls. At last, it was resolved to storm the place. The attack was made by Montgomery and Anold at different points. It was a desperate attempt to make with only nine hundred effective men.

4. In spite of a blinding snow-storm, the Americans advanced bravely to the assault. But it was in vain. Montgomery was shot down at the head of his men. Arnold was disabled by a bullet in the leg. The muskets of many of the Americans were rendered useless by the snow. One party were obliged to surrender on the spot. The rest continued the siege till they heard that a powerful British army was approaching. Then they hastily retreated; and soon all Canada was again in the hands of the British.

5. The King and Parliament found it was not so easy to conquer "the rebels" as they had expected. So they sent to Germany, and hired a number of Hessians, as they were called, to come and fight for them. In the mean time, Congress was busy in collecting stores and buying powder. They urged Washington to attack the British at Boston, with the force collected under his command at Cambridge. But ammunition was scarce; the men, brave as they

were, needed discipline; so that Washington did not think it prudent to take the field till the spring of 1776.

6. Dorchester Heights command the city and harbor of Boston. Early in March, General Washington sent a body of men by night to throw up intrenchments there. It was hard work, for the ground was frozen. The Americans, however, plied their pick-axes diligently, and by morning had raised a strong breastwork of earth. When the British general saw what had been done, he determined to dislodge the enemy. But a storm set in, and before it ceased the Americans had fortified themselves so strongly that he was afraid to make the attempt.

7. As the cannon on Dorchester Heights swept the whole of Boston, the British army had to leave, or *evacuate*, the city. They sailed away in their ships, to the great joy of the patriots. Those who had remained in the city during the siege had suffered much. Besides being insulted and maltreated by the soldiers, they could hardly get food to eat or wood to keep them warm. After first sailing to the north, the British general landed his men on Staten Island, with the view of attacking New York. Washington had already reached the city and prepared for its defence.

QUESTIONS.—1. What did Congress proceed to carry on? What was their object in invading Canada? To whom did they give the command of the expedition? What places surrendered? What place remained? What difficulty did Montgomery now meet with?—2. Who were at this time making their way to join Montgomery? Give an account of the sufferings of Arnold's party.—3. When this party arrived, what did Montgomery do? What success did he meet with in the siege? At last, what desperate resolve was formed?—4. Give an account of the attack on Quebec. What was one party of the Americans obliged to do? What was done by the rest? How long did they remain before Quebec?—5. Whom did the King and Parliament hire to fight for them in America? In the mean time, what was Congress doing? What did they urge Washington to do? Why was he unwilling to attack the British? When did he take the field?—6. What was Washington's first movement? What did the British general determine to do?

What prevented him from making the attempt?—7. What were the British then obliged to do? How did the patriots feel at this? How had those patriots who had stayed in Boston suffered? Where did the British go? Who had preceded them?

LESSON XXXII.

ATTACK ON CHARLESTON.—DECLARATION OF INDEPENDENCE

Sergeant Jasper raising the flag at Fort Moultrie.

1. In June, 1776, the people of South Carolina heard that a strong British fleet, with a large army on board, was about to at-

tack Charleston. They quickly erected a fort of palmetto-wood and earth, and garrisoned it with brave men under Colonel Moultrie. They did not have to wait long for the enemy. One British ship came up after another, and soon a heavy fire was opened on the fort. But it did little harm. Palmetto-wood is soft; and the balls, instead of splitting or tearing it, sank into it without doing any injury.

2. It was not so, however, with the fire from the fort. This did fearful execution on the British ships. At one time, the quarter-deck of the admiral's vessel was cleared of every man except the admiral himself. The troops on board landed, and tried to reach the fort, but were driven back. At last, having kept up the attack for nine hours without any success, the British were obliged to retire. They suffered much in the action; the Americans, but little.

3. In the midst of the battle, a British ball struck the flag-staff of the fort. The flag was carried away, and fell in front of the fort, on the beach. Then a brave heart showed its courage. Sergeant Jasper, amid the balls that rained from the British vessels, leaped over the rampart, ran along the beach, and secured the flag. Then fastening it to the sponge-staff of a cannon, he again raised it over the fort amid the cheers of his companions. After the battle, Governor Rutledge presented him his own sword for this gallant deed.

4. Jasper was afterwards of great service to the American army. He acted as a scout, and brought them information about the British. He was once scouting with a single companion, when he saw a party of ten British soldiers taking some prisoners to Savannah. It was said that the prisoners were to be hung, and Jasper determined to save them. For some time the two Americans kept on the track of the party, without seeing any chance of attempting a rescue. At last they drew near Savannah. Two miles from the city was a fa-

mous spring, and here the British, with their prisoners, stopped for a drink.

5. Two of the party were left on guard, while the rest laid aside their guns and went down to the spring. This was the moment Jasper and his companion had waited for. Shooting down the soldiers on duty, and knocking over several others with their clubbed muskets, they obtained possession of the loaded guns of the British. The latter had to yield to their two brave enemies. The rescued Americans were then unbound, and armed with the guns of their guard; and Jasper and his men marched off in triumph with their prisoners.

6. The 4th of July is always kept as a great holiday in the United States. Do you know why it is kept? Because on the 4th of July, 1776, the Continental Congress adopted a Declaration of Independence. Up to this time they had hoped that the King and Parliament would give up their unjust claims. In that case, they would have laid down their arms, and remained subjects of Great Britain. But now, following the example set by the brave people of Charlotte, they said the King should rule over them no more. They boldly declared their independence, and pledged their lives and fortunes for its support. After this, the thirteen colonies were called " the Thirteen United States of America ".

7. While Congress was discussing the Declaration, the streets of Philadelphia were filled with crowds, anxious to know what it would do. When the **old bell-ringer** pealed the bell of the statehouse, as a signal that **the bill had passed,** their joy knew no bounds. Bonfires were lighted, and houses illuminated. In New York, the people showed their delight by pulling down a great leaden statue of the King, and moulding it into bullets to fire against his soldiers. In Boston, the Declaration was read at a public meeting, amid the

cheers of thousands. Here is a picture of Independence Hall, in Philadelphia, the building in which Congress met and the Declaration of Independence was signed.

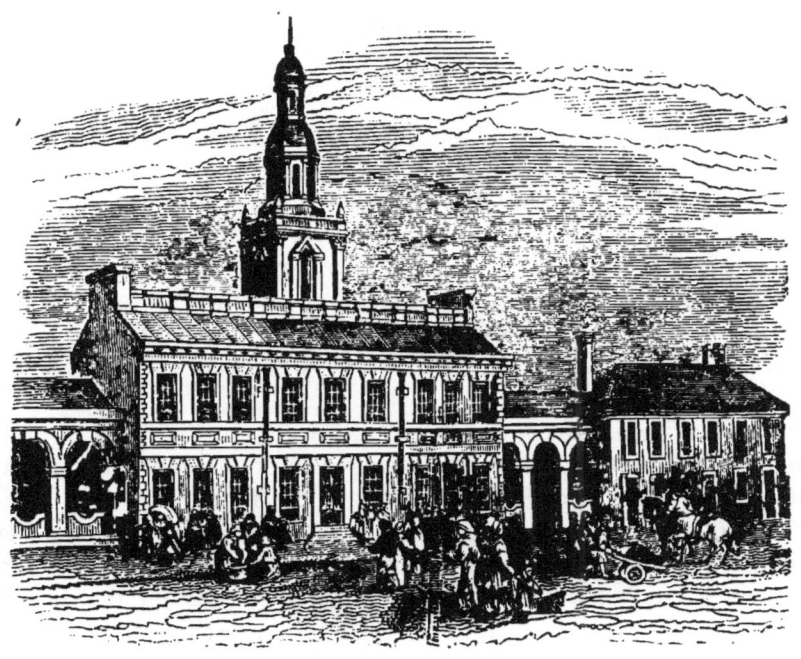

QUESTIONS.—1. What did the people of South Carolina hear in June, 1776? What did they do, on learning this? What soon appeared? What was the effect of the British fire on the fort?—2. What was the effect of the fire from the fort? What is said of the admiral's vessel? What attempt was made by the troops? How long did the British keep up the attack? What was the result?—3. What gallant deed was performed by Sergeant Jasper in this battle?—4, 5. Tell the story about Jasper's rescuing some American prisoners near Savannah.—6. Why is the 4th of July kept as a holiday? What had Congress hoped? On the 4th of July, 1776, what did Congress do? After this, what were the thirteen colonies styled?—7. What took place in Philadelphia, while Congress was discussing the Declaration? How was the news that the Declaration had passed received in New York? How, in Boston? What is represented in the engraving?

LESSON XXXII.

BATTLE OF LONG ISLAND.

1. In the summer of 1776, New York became the centre of the war. General Howe was now the British commander. Besides the men who had been driven from Boston, he had many fresh troops just from Europe. Among the rest were a large number of Hessians. With these he advanced on New York by way of Long Island. The Americans had thrown up fortifications at the west end of the island, opposite New York, where the city of Brooklyn now stands. Nine thousand men were sent over, to keep the British in check.

2. The British army advanced in three divisions. One of these, making a circuit over the hills, managed to get behind the advanced detachments that had been thrown out by the Americans. While the patriots were busily engaged with the enemy in front, they were dismayed to hear a firing in their rear. They soon saw that they were surrounded. A few fought their way through the British, and reached the American lines. Many fell; a still greater number were made prisoners. Howe advanced to within a short distance of the fortifications, but, instead of attacking them, waited for his fleet to come up.

3. During the battle, Washington crossed from New York. He saw his best troops falling, without the power to help them. He could only hope to save those who remained by a timely retreat. On the third night after the battle, while Howe was still waiting

for his fleet, the whole American army embarked in boats, and, with their baggage and stores, were conveyed to New York. A thick fog concealed their movements; the boats were rowed with muffled oars; and the British had no idea of what was going on till the Americans were beyond their reach.

4. A woman living near the river saw the Americans embarking, and sent a negro to inform the British. Fortunately, he fell into the hands of the Hessians, who could not understand what he said. Had it not been for this, the whole army might have been captured. The battle of Long Island was most disastrous to the American cause. Numbers deserted from the army; and many who were before in doubt which side to join, now decided in favor of the King.

5. On first approaching the city, Howe had sent a letter to Washington, for the purpose of conciliating the Americans. Washington refused to receive it, because Howe would not acknowledge him as commander of the American army. After the battle of Long Island, Howe made a second attempt. A committee of Congress met him. They found he had no authority to recognize their independence, but could only grant them pardon, and receive them back as subjects of Great Britain. They wanted no pardon, and were determined never to be subjects of Great Britain. So nothing was effected.

6. Some of the people of New York were opposed to the Revolution. They were called Tories, while those who favored it were known as Whigs. While Washington was in New York, about this time, several tories formed a plot to poison him. They bribed one of his guard to put some arsenic in a dish of peas prepared for his dinner. The plot was revealed to Washington through a young girl who had overheard it.

7. To discover the guilty party, Washington had a trusty soldier disguised as a servant, and sent him into the kitchen to watch the peas. He had not been there long, before he saw one of his comrades come anxiously to the door and look in. Presently he entered, and hesitating, as if horror-struck at the act, sprinkled a powder in the pot in which the peas were cooking. Washington was at once informed of this. At dinner, when he had seated himself among his officers, he asked them to wait for a moment, and ordered in his guard.

8. Fixing his eyes on the guilty man, he put a spoonful of peas on his plate, and asked him, "Shall I eat of these?" "I don't know," stammered the man, turning deadly pale. Washington took some on his knife, and again asked, "Shall I eat of these?" The man could not say a word, but raised his hand as if to prevent it. A chicken was brought in, and fed with some of the peas; it died on the spot. This proved that they had been poisoned. The man was carried fainting from the room, and Washington was saved.

9. This same year, a British sloop-of-war put into the island called Martha's Vineyard. It was in want of a spar, and the only stick of timber there that would answer the purpose was a liberty-tree, erected by the patriots. This tree the captain said he must have; but three brave girls, not yet sixteen years old, said he should not have it. The night before it was to be cut down, they went in the dark, bored several holes in the tree, and filled them with gunpowder. Then, lighting a slow-match, they blew the tree to pieces. So his Majesty's sloop-of-war had to go without a spar.

QUESTIONS.—1. Where did the war centre in 1776? Who was now the British commander? What troops had Howe? In what direction did he advance on New York? What preparations had the Americans made on Long Island?—2. Give an account of

[1776] WASHINGTON'S RETREAT FROM NEW YORK.

the battle of Long Island. After the battle, why did not Howe attack the American fortifications?—3. Who crossed to Long Island during the battle? Tell how Washington saved the army.—4. How did the British come near learning that the Americans were embarking? What was the effect of the battle of Long Island?—5. What had Howe done on first approaching New York? How were his advances met? What passed between Howe and a committee of Congress after the battle?—6. Who were called Tories, and who Whigs? What plot was formed by the Tories? How did Washington hear of it?—7. What measures were taken by Washington to discover the guilty party?—8. What passed at dinner?—9. Tell the story about the sloop-of-war that put into Martha's Vineyard.

LESSON XXXIV.

WASHINGTON'S RETREAT.—TRENTON.—PRINCETON.

1. We left Washington in New York. His army was discouraged by the defeat on Long Island. One-fourth of the men were sick. He could not hope to repel the British, who were preparing to cross from Long Island and attack the city. The only course left him was to retreat, and accordingly he drew off his men to the north. The British immediately took possession of the city. They retained it till the end of the war. Howe, with most of the army, kept on in pursuit of Washington.

2. Washington hardly felt strong enough to risk a battle. He retreated as the enemy advanced, but so slowly that frequent skirmishes took place. At last a battle was fought at White Plains, without any decided advantage to either party. After this, Washington took his army across the Hudson River to New Jersey, leaving nearly three thousand of his best men in Fort Washington. The British made a spirited attack on this post, and the garrison had to surrender. Washington is said to have wept, as from the other side of the river he saw his men falling beneath the British bayonets.

3. The loss of Fort Washington and its garrison was the heaviest blow the patriots had yet received. Lord Cornwallis [*corn-wol'-lis*] immediately set out in pursuit of the American army, now much reduced in size. Sadly this little band retreated across New Jersey. Many of them, ragged and barefooted, left their blood-stained tracks on the frozen ground. The British pressed on hotly in pursuit. But Washington reached the Delaware River, secured all the boats for many miles, and went over into Pennsylvania with his suffering men. Unable to cross the Delaware, Cornwallis resolved to wait till it should be frozen over. Dividing his army, he stationed detachments at Trenton, Princeton, and other points.

4. Washington now saw he must do something to encourage his men. He resolved to cross the Delaware and surprise a large body of Hessians stationed at Trenton. Christmas night was chosen for the attempt, as a time when they would likely be carousing, and

off their guard. The night was dark and bitterly cold. The Delaware was full of ice. Part of the Americans, however, succeeded in getting across. They completely surprised the Hessians, a thousand of whom at once threw down their arms.

5. Washington durst not remain at Trenton, for he knew the British from the posts around would soon be upon him. So he immediately recrossed into Pennsylvania with his prisoners. On the opposite page you see him and his men toiling through the snow. In gaining this glorious victory, he lost only four men, two of whom were frozen to death. The British, who had thought the Revolution was almost at an end, now found they were mistaken.

6. A few days after this victory, Washington again crossed the Delaware to Trenton. Cornwallis, anxious for a battle, soon made his appearance. Night was near at hand, and, after some skirmishing, both parties rested on their arms. Washington felt he was no match for Cornwallis, and determined to disappoint him. Leaving his fires burning, and posting a sentinel here and there, to deceive the enemy, he noiselessly withdrew his men in the night, and marched to Princeton, to surprise the British stationed there. When Cornwallis woke the next morning, he could see no enemy. He had been outgeneralled.

7. Washington did not surprise the British at Princeton, for he met them already on the march to join Cornwallis. A battle ensued. At first the Americans, having no bayonets, gave way. But Washington placed himself before the advancing British, and his men rallied to support their beloved chief. The British were repulsed. Washington had gained another victory. He led his men, exhausted as they were by want of food and sleep, to Morristown, and there fixed his winter-quarters.

8. Washington's men suffered much at Morristown from cold and sickness, during the winter of 1777. The small-pox broke

out among them, and many died. The people of the place were true patriots, and did all they could to relieve the suffering soldiers. They gave them the best they had, saying, "Nothing is too good for those who fight for our country." Washington sent out several expeditions in the course of the winter, and recovered nearly the whole of Jersey.

9. Cornwallis's army was much larger than Washington's. It was feared if he knew this, he would fall upon Morristown. So the Americans had recourse to a stratagem to deceive him. There was a man in the camp, whom they suspected of being a British spy. A false statement was made out of the men and ammunition at Morristown, representing the Americans as much better off than they really were. An officer, as if by chance, left the paper on a table by which the suspected spy was sitting, and went out for a few moments. On his return, both the paper and the spy were missing. They no doubt found their way to Cornwallis, and misled him as to the strength of the Americans.

QUESTIONS.—1. What was the state of the American army in New York after the battle of Long Island? What was Washington obliged to do? What then became of New York? What course did Howe pursue?—2. Describe Washington's movements. Where did a battle take place? With what result? What did Washington then do? What took place at Fort Washington?—3. What followed the fall of Fort Washington? Describe the retreat of the American army across New Jersey. How did Washington save his men? What did Cornwallis do, on arriving at the Delaware?—4. What was the next movement of Washington? What time was chosen for the attempt, and why? Give an account of the surprise of the Hessians at Trenton.—5. What was done by Washington after the surprise at Trenton? How many men had he lost?—6. A few days afterwards, what movement did Washington make? Who soon appeared, to give him battle? Tell how Washington disappointed Cornwallis.—7. What took place at Princeton? Where did Washington fix his winter-quarters?—8. From what did the Americans suffer at Morristown? How did the people of the place treat them? What did Washington accomplish during the winter?—9. Relate the stratagem by which Cornwallis was misled as to the strength of the Americans.

LESSON XXXV.

BURGOYNE'S CAMPAIGN.

1. In 1777, another powerful British army took the field, under the command of General Burgoyne. Starting from Canada, Burgoyne invaded the state of New York. On the bank of Lake Champlain, he gave a great war-feast to a number of Indians, many of whom joined his army. Ticonderoga and Fort Edward were taken in succession. The Americans who had garrisoned these posts fell back as Burgoyne advanced. To delay his march, bridges were broken down, and the roads obstructed.

2. The northern American army was commanded by General Schuyler [*ski'-ler*]. One night, when the general was preparing to retire to bed in his own house, a servant, passing into the room, caught a glimpse of a figure concealed behind the door. Pretending not to notice it, she managed to tell her master in an undertone what she had seen. An alarm was raised. The party fled, but was overtaken by the guard. It was an Indian, who had hidden himself behind the door to murder the general.

3. Before leaving Canada, Burgoyne had sent a large detachment to overrun the western part of New York. This force met with a brave resistance at Fort Stanwix. The American general, Herkimer, advanced with some militia-men to relieve this fort. He fell into an ambuscade, and, early in the action, received a wound in the leg. Seated on a hillock, he continued to give his orders. While the enemy's balls were falling round him, he coolly drew his pipe from his pocket, lighted it, and commenced smoking, while he directed the movements of his men. They fought bravely, but were utterly defeated.

4. The fort still held out, and Arnold, with a detachment from Schuyler's army, undertook to relieve it. When a short distance from the British, Arnold contrived to get a report spread among them that a large body of Americans was within a few hours' march of their camp. A panic seized them, and regulars, tories, and Indians, were soon in full flight. Tents, baggage, provisions, and artillery, were left behind. The besieging force was broken up, and the fort was saved.

5. A second detachment was sent by Burgoyne to Bennington, Vermont, to capture the stores deposited there. General Stark met them with some brave militia-men, hastily collected. When he saw the British forming for battle, Stark thus addressed his troops: "See, men! There are the red-coats. We must beat them to-day, or Molly Stark's a widow!" And they did beat. Six hundred of the British were taken prisoners.

6. Among Stark's men was a minister, who wanted to fight, but had conscientious scruples about doing so till he had invited the enemy to surrender. So, going near their camp before the battle, he commenced preaching to them, and urging them to lay down their arms. A volley of musketry was the reply. "Now give me a gun," said the minister to a friend who had accompanied him. The way he handled his gun in the battle showed that he had quite got over his conscientious scruples.

7. Burgoyne had depended much on these two expeditions. Their failure was a severe blow. The Indians became discouraged and departed. The tories were afraid to join him. Provisions became scarce. The Americans carefully removed their cattle and every thing that could be of use to his army. Mrs. Schuyler, by her husband's orders, set fire to her own fields of grain, to prevent their falling into the hands of the enemy. Here you see her apply-

ing the torch. Meanwhile, the farmers of New York and New England were pouring into the American camp.

8. Just at this time, Congress unjustly removed Schuyler from the command of the northern army, and appointed General Gates in his stead. Gates determined to make a stand on the west bank of the Hudson, and erected fortifications there. Burgoyne could go no farther without giving battle. This he resolved to do. On the 19th of September, 1777, the first battle of Stillwater was fought. The action was most severe and lasted till night. Though neither party gained a decided victory, the Americans had the advantage.

9. Burgoyne was now in greater danger than ever. He had sent for aid to the British general at New York, but had received no answer. Again he must either starve or fight. He resolved on

another engagement, and on the 7th of October the second battle of Stillwater took place. This time the Americans were completely victorious. Morgan, with his riflemen, and Arnold, whom you have heard of before, repelled the furious charges of the British, and drove them from their ground. In vain Burgoyne strove to rally his men. The Americans were left in possession of the field.

10. As soon as night set in, Burgoyne fell back on Saratoga. He hoped to be able to retreat. But it was too late; he was hemmed in on all sides. His messages to General Clinton were still unanswered. No other course was left than to surrender. This he did. All his men, nearly six thousand in number, laid down their arms, and gave up their baggage, cannon, and ammunition at Saratoga. What rejoicings there were throughout the country over the glorious news that Burgoyne's great army had surrendered to the "rebels" it had come to crush!

QUESTIONS.—1. In 1777, who led another British army into the field? What state did Burgoyne invade? What did he do on the bank of Lake Champlain? What posts were taken? What did the Americans do as Burgoyne advanced?—2. Who commanded the northern American army? Give an account of the attempt to murder General Schuyler.—3. What detachment had been sent out by Burgoyne? Where did this detachment meet with a brave resistance? Give an account of General Herkimer's attempt to relieve Fort Stanwix.—4. Who then undertook to relieve the fort? Relate Arnold's stratagem.—5. Where did Burgoyne send another detachment? By whom were they met? How did Stark address his men? What was the result of the battle of Bennington?—6. Relate the story about the conscientious minister.—7. What effect did the failure of these expeditions have? What is related of Mrs. Schuyler? How was the American army increased?—8. What change was now made in the command of the northern army? What did Gates determine to do? What was the consequence? Give an account of the first battle of Stillwater.—9. What was now Burgoyne's condition? Give an account of the second battle of Stillwater.—10. What was Burgoyne's next movement? What was he finally obliged to do? What were surrendered at Saratoga?

LESSON XXXVI.

BRANDYWINE.—GERMANTOWN.—VALLEY FORGE.

1. While these events were going on in the north, Washington was trying to keep General Howe in check. Unable to bring Washington to an engagement in New Jersey, Howe had put to sea with eighteen thousand men. He landed about fifty miles from Philadelphia, and commenced marching towards that city. Congress was in session at Philadelphia, and Washington wanted to save the city if he could. He had only eight thousand men fit for service, but with these he met the British at Brandywine. The Americans were defeated. Congress had to leave Philadelphia. Howe entered the city in triumph.

2. Among those who fought bravely at Brandywine was La Fayette [*lah fa-et'*]. This young French noble had left his home and friends, and come over to help the Americans fight for freedom. His family objected to his coming. But La Fayette, without their knowledge, bought a vessel, and with a few noble hearts like himself succeeded in reaching America. Congress made him a general, and he became the bosom friend of Washington.

3. The British were now in pleasant quarters in and around Philadelphia. A large division was stationed at Germantown, six miles from the city. This force Washington tried to surprise, October 4th, 1777. At first victory inclined to the Americans. But some of the men failed to obey orders, and a thick fog arose, which gave the British a chance to rally. The Americans were defeated with considerable loss. Cold weather soon set in, and Washington led his men into winter-quarters at Valley Forge, about twenty miles from Philadelphia.

4. An amusing incident took place at the battle of Germantown. General Greene, who commanded one division of the Americans, had by his side a major, who wore his hair down his back in a cue. While the firing was at its height, a bullet carried off the major's cue. "Don't be in a hurry, major," said Greene; "just get down and pick up your cue." The major very coolly did so. Presently another ball came along, and cut off one of General Greene's curls. "Now, general," said the major, "it's your turn. Just dismount and get your curl." But the general preferred letting his curl go.

5. Washington's men suffered intensely at Valley Forge. A great part of them could not move out of their huts for want of clothes. Many had no shoes. Some were without blankets, and had to rest at night in their rags on the bare frozen ground. Sickness set in. Food could hardly be obtained. Most of the people

The American Army at Valley Forge.

in the neighborhood were tories, who sold their produce to the British at high prices. Washington had no gold or silver, and the paper money issued by Congress was worth but little. This was indeed a trying hour.

6. There were some kind hearts, however, that felt for the poor American soldiers. One devoted woman, Mary Knight, used to cook provisions for them, and carry them herself to the camp in the depth of winter, disguised as a market-woman, that she might pass the British outposts. Her brother was a general in the American army. The British set a price upon his head; but this brave woman saved him by heading him up in an empty cider hogshead in the cellar, and feeding him through the bunghole. He stayed there three days, and the British searched the house four times for him without success.

7. While things looked thus gloomy, a joyful piece of news reached the camp. It was that France had acknowledged the independence of the United States, and would help them against England. This was brought about chiefly through the efforts of Benjamin Franklin. This great man was the son of a candle-maker. In his youth, his father employed him in cutting wicks and filling candle-moulds. But he longed for knowledge. He would even deny himself sleep that he might read and study. After learning the art of printing, he left his home and set out to make his fortune.

8. Franklin found himself in Philadelphia with a single dollar in his pocket. For a time he had hard work to get along. But he was very frugal. He lived on gruel; and, when his landlady informed him she could not afford to board him any longer at the price he was paying, he told her she must make the gruel thinner. Franklin became a great writer and philosopher. His name was

honored in Europe, and in his own country he was revered as a true-hearted patriot.

QUESTIONS.—1. While Burgoyne was conducting his campaign, what was Washington trying to do? What movements had been made by Howe? How many men had each general? Where did they meet? What was the result of the battle of Brandywine?—
—2. Who is mentioned as fighting bravely at Brandywine? What is said of this young French noble?—3. Where was a large division of the British stationed? What attempt did Washington make? Give an account of the battle of Germantown. Where did Washington lead his men into winter-quarters?—4. What amusing incident took place during the battle of Germantown?—5. What was the condition of the American army at Valley Forge? What made it hard for them to get provisions?—6. How did Mary Knight help the American soldiers? How did she preserve her brother?—7. Amid the general gloom, what joyful news was received? By whose efforts had this been brought about? What is said of the youth of Benjamin Franklin?—8. On reaching Philadelphia, what did Franklin find? What passed between him and his landlady? How was Franklin regarded?

LESSON XXXVII.

MONMOUTH.—WYOMING.—MOVEMENTS IN THE SOUTH.

1. In the spring of 1778, Howe returned to England, and General Clinton took command of the British forces. Clinton had orders to evacuate Philadelphia and lead his men to New York. To do this, he had to cross New Jersey. Washington was soon in pursuit. His army was not half so large as Clinton's, and most of his officers thought it would be imprudent to risk an engagement. Washington thought otherwise; and at Monmouth, New Jersey, he gave battle to Clinton.

2. General Lee was to commence the attack with an advanced division. What was Washington's dismay, when, on coming up with the main force, he found this division retreating without having struck a blow. He at once stopped them, and posted his men

in such a way that the British were checked. The action continued till night with advantage to the Americans. They rested on their arms, expecting to renew the battle in the morning. Washington slept on the field in his cloak. But, when day dawned, no British were to be seen. They had silently departed for New York.

3. On the day of the battle the heat was intense. Many of the British soldiers died from its effects. When Monmouth is mentioned, the name of Molly Pitcher must not be forgotten. Her husband served at one of the American cannon. While she was bringing him water from a spring, a ball struck him, and he fell. There was no one to manage his gun. Springing forward, she took his place, and performed her duty in the most heroic manner. Washington appointed her a sergeant in the army, and she was afterwards well known as " Captain Molly ".

4. The Indians, bribed by the British, had from time to time during the war given trouble on the frontier. In the summer of 1778, in company with a band of tories, they made a descent on Wy-o'-ming. This was a flourishing settlement in a lovely valley in Pennsylvania. Most of the men were away, fighting for their country. Those who remained, hearing of their danger, quickly armed themselves, and assembled in a fort with the women and children. When the tories and Indians were near the fort, they sent word to the officer in command to come out and confer with them.

5. Taking some of his men as a guard, he did as they requested, but was immediately attacked. Most of the party were cut off. The next day, the enemy surrounded the fort. After holding out till most of his men had fallen, the commander surrendered, on the promise that those within should be spared. But no sooner were the tories and Indians admitted than they commenced killing all

they met. Some even murdered their own relatives. Wyoming was a ruin. Few of its once happy people escaped the massacre.

6. Late in the year 1778, the British commenced operations in the south. They took Savannah, and overran the eastern part of Georgia, robbing the whig families, and spreading terror in their path. A French fleet containing a body of troops having arrived off the coast, General Lincoln hastened to join them in attacking Savannah. The French would not wait to besiege the city; so it was resolved to storm it. Though the attack was bravely made, the Americans and French were driven back with loss. The brave Jasper lost his life in trying to save the flag of his regiment.

7. The patriots of the south suffered a still more serious reverse the next year. A strong force of British collected around Charleston, which was defended by General Lincoln, with a large army. The Americans held out till their houses were nearly battered down by the British cannon, but were obliged to yield at last. Five thousand men, with stores and artillery, thus fell into the hands of the enemy.

8. One of the British posts in Georgia was held by a Captain French, with forty men and five vessels. Colonel White, with four men, set out to capture them. Near the British post they kindled a number of fires, as if a large camp were there, and then, quickly riding round, gave various orders in a loud tone of voice, as if they were directing the movements of a large army. They completely deceived Captain French, who thought there was no use of attempting to resist such a host, and surrendered his men and vessels.

9. But how were the five men to secure their prisoners? There was danger that the latter would discover the artifice, and overwhelm them with numbers. So Colonel White told them that his men were very angry at the British on account of their outrages, and that they had better keep out of sight. He would send them

ahead with three or four of his men as guides, while he remained to restrain his army. Then, hastening off, he collected the militia of the neighborhood, who soon overtook the others, and led the British in triumph to the nearest American post.

QUESTIONS.—1. In 1778, what change was made in the command of the British army? What orders had Clinton? How did his army compare with Washington's? Where did they meet?—2. Give an account of the battle of Monmouth. How did the Americans and Washington pass the night? What did they find in the morning?—3. Describe the weather on the day of the battle. Tell the story of Molly Pitcher.—4. What is said of the Indians on the frontier? What did they do in 1778? Where was Wyoming? What preparations were made by its inhabitants? What message did the enemy send to the commanding officer?—5. What befell this officer and his guard? What followed? Give an account of the massacre.—6. Where did the British commence operations, towards the close of 1778? What city did they take? By whom were they attacked in Savannah? What was the result of the attack? Who lost his life in this battle?—7. What serious reverse did the patriots of the south suffer the next year? What fell into the hands of the enemy at Charleston?—8. Relate the stratagem practised by Colonel White?—9. How did White secure his prisoners.

LESSON XXXVIII.

PAUL JONES.—FRANCIS MARION.

1. On the ocean, the United States could do but little against the great navy of England. Many fast-sailing little vessels, however, were armed and sent out by private persons. They were called *privateers*. Cruising wherever there was a chance of taking a prize, they were of great service in cutting off English merchant-vessels, capturing stores, &c. Congress managed from time to time to procure a few vessels. These were intrusted to skilful commanders, who gained some important victories. Among the most famous of these commanders was Paul Jones.

2. Paul Jones was the son of a Scottish gardener. From early boyhood he was fond of the sea. After making various voyages, he settled in Virginia. When the Revolution broke out, he walked to Philadelphia and offered his services to Congress. They were accepted, and he had the honor of hoisting the first flag that ever floated over an American man-of-war. It was of yellow silk, and bore the device of a pine tree and a rattlesnake, with the words *Don't tread on me.* Jones was soon off to Nova Scotia, running into the harbors, destroying the shipping, and capturing prizes.

3. Jones afterwards cruised about the English coasts, to repay the enemy for their outrages in American ports. He was so successful in his descents that his very name became a terror. At one point of the coast, when his dreaded vessel was seen in the offing, the minister went down with his congregation to the shore, and made a strange but fervent prayer for deliverance. Soon afterwards the wind rose, white caps appeared on the sea, and Jones had to change his course,—owing, as the people believed, to their minister's prayer.

4. Jones' most famous battle was with the British frigate Ser'-a-pis (September, 1779). After one of the most terrible actions ever fought, the British struck their colors. Finding his vessel sinking, Jones took his men on board of the Serapis. She was on fire, but he succeeded in saving her. The captain of the Serapis was made a knight by the King for his bravery in this battle. "Well, he deserved it," said Paul Jones; "and, if I fall in with him again, I'll make a lord of him."

5. During the winter of 1778–9, General Putnam was stationed with some troops in Connecticut. Early one morning, while shaving, he saw in the looking-glass a body of red-coats coming up the road. Throwing down his razor, he buckled on his sword, mounted

his horse, and roused his men. But they were too few to oppose the enemy, and the order was given to retreat.

6. The soldiers fled in different directions. Putnam found himself, hotly pursued by some dragoons, at the top of a steep descent, consisting of about a hundred steps, cut in the rock for the convenience of those who attended church on the hill. Down this perilous descent he dashed, turning to wave defiance at the dragoons, who durst not follow. They fired at him, but he escaped with a bullet through his hat.

7. We left the British in possession of Savannah and Charleston. Sending out parties, they soon overran the whole of South Carolina. The people were required to acknowledge the King's authority. But

even those who did so were often robbed and driven from their homes. Such outrages roused many of the brave people of Carolina. They formed small parties, took to the swamps and woods, and resolved to fight till their country was free. Wherever a British detachment was to be cut off, or a band of tories to be dispersed, they appeared when least expected. They often went into battle with only three charges of powder apiece. Some were without guns, and would have to wait for those of their companions who fell.

8. No braver men ever lived than the leaders of these parties. Among them were Sumter, called from his courage " the Carolina Game-cock ", and Marion, the cunning " Swamp Fox ". Marion was one of the heroes of the palmetto fort. He was also in Charleston under Lincoln, and escaped being taken by a singular accident. Shortly after the enemy appeared, he was dining with some friends, who insisted on his drinking with them to excess. To avoid doing so, he jumped to the street from the second-story window, and broke his ankle. Unfit for duty, he was conveyed from the city by a road that was still open, and thus escaped to serve his country.

9. Marion and his men were the terror of the British and tories. They seemed to rest neither day nor night. Making their home in forests which the enemy could not penetrate, they lived on what scanty food they could there procure. A British officer once visited Marion, to arrange for an exchange of prisoners. He was invited to stay to dinner, and presently a few roasted sweet potatoes were brought in on a shingle. The officer could hardly believe that this was all his dreaded enemy had to live on. On his return, he resigned his commission in the British army, saying that such men could not be subdued.

10. The high-souled women of Carolina did their part also. They tried to provide their brave defenders with clothes, and keep

them informed of the enemy's movements. To save a party of whigs, a Miss Moore, only fifteen years old, set out in a boat at night, with her little brother and a female friend, and, after rowing for miles at the risk of her life, delivered her message and returned. In one district, a company of young women went round in harvest time to the different farms, and, wherever they found that the owner was away, fighting for his country, they cut and garnered his grain.

QUESTIONS.—1. How did the power of the United States compare with that of England on the ocean? What are privateers? How did they annoy the English? Who was among the most famous officers employed by Congress?—2. Give an account of the early life of Paul Jones. What did he do when the Revolution broke out? What honor did he enjoy? Describe this flag. What was Jones soon doing?—3. Where did Jones afterwards cruise? How was he looked upon? What happened at one point of the coast? —4. What was Jones' most famous battle? What was the result of the engagement? What honor did the King confer on the commander of the Serapis? What did Jones say?—5, 6. Give an account of Putnam's escape from the dragoons.—7. What state was overrun by the British in 1780? What were the people required to do? What outrages were committed? What was their effect?—8. Name two famous partisan leaders. Where had Marion served? How had he escaped capture at Charleston?—9. What is said of Marion and his men? Relate the story of Marion and the British officer.—10. How did the women of Carolina help their defenders? Tell the story of Miss Moore. What was done by one company of young women?

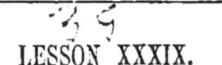

LESSON XXXIX.

HANGING ROCK.—CAMDEN.—ARNOLD'S TREASON.

1. Marion and his men met with many an adventure. The famous leader was once nearly surrounded in a corn-field by British dragoons. His only chance of escape lay in leaping a fence seven feet high, with a wide ditch beyond it. The dragoons thought they had caught the Swamp Fox at last. What was their surprise, when

his horse made the leap in gallant style, cleared fence and ditch, and bore his master safely off into an adjoining thicket!

Marion and his Men.

2. Among Marion's bravest followers were Colonel Horry and Captain Baxter. In one of their battles, Baxter cried out, "I am wounded, colonel." "No matter, Baxter," answered Horry; "stand to your post." "But I can't stand," said Baxter; "I am wounded a second time." "Lie down, then, captain, but quit not your post." "They have shot me again," cried Baxter; "and, if I stay here any longer, I shall be shot to pieces." "Well, Baxter, be it so, but stir not," was Horry's reply:—and the order was obeyed, though the wounded man was shot a fourth time during the battle.

3. At last Congress sent an army to the south, under General

Gates. Gates marched towards Camden, one of the chief posts of the British. As he approached, the hopes of the patriots revived. A number of farmers took the field, and defeated a large detachment of the enemy at Hanging Rock.

4. The powder used by the Americans in this battle had been stored in a house occupied by one of the patriots, with his wife and mother-in-law. Shortly before the battle, a party of British surrounded the house, and commenced attacking it. The two women loaded guns, while the man fired them, with such rapidity that the British thought a large body of troops was posted there, and gave up the attack. Thus the powder was saved.

5. On the 15th of August, 1780, Gates drew up his men, and late at night set out for Camden to surprise the enemy. Strangely enough, the British, without knowing of this movement, were on the march to surprise Gates. The two armies met and joined battle. Early in the engagement, some of the Americans gave way, and the result was a total defeat. Great quantities of stores were taken by the British. Gates could not rally his men. His army was completely broken up. Shortly after this, Congress removed Gates from the command of the southern army, and appointed General Greene in his stead.

6. The whole state was now at the mercy of the English. Congress wanted to send an army into the field, but could not do so for want of funds. They had kept issuing paper money; and now there was so much of it out that people lost faith in its value, and it passed for very little. It took six hundred dollars of it to buy a pair of boots. The pay of an officer would hardly keep his horse in oats. It is not strange that Congress found it hard to raise soldiers.

7. Meanwhile, Washington's army in the north was in so wretched a state that he could do nothing. Every thing looked

gloomy; and, to make matters worse, a treacherous blow was just at this time aimed at the patriot cause. Arnold, whose bravery at Quebec and Stillwater you have read of, became a traitor. He was in command of a strong fortress that had been built by the Americans at West Point. This post he offered to betray to the British, on condition that they would make him a general in their army, and give him about fifty thousand dollars.

8. Major Andre, an accomplished British officer, was sent up from New York to arrange the terms with Arnold. He came within the American lines, and, having agreed with the traitor and received the necessary papers, set out on his return. When he had almost reached the British outposts, he was stopped by three American militia-men. On examining him, they found the papers in his stockings. Refusing an offer of ten thousand guineas to let him go, these honest patriots took their prisoner to the nearest American post. After a fair trial, he was hanged as a spy.

9. Arnold heard of Andre's capture in time to escape to a British vessel. Receiving his promised rank in the British army, he afterwards showed his hatred of the patriots by ravaging different parts of the country. But British as well as Americans despised him. He enjoys the honor of being the only traitor in the Revolutionary War.

10. Washington was very anxious to capture the traitor, and a plan was formed for that purpose. A Virginian pretended to desert, and joined Arnold's legion. The traitor's quarters were then in New York, near the Hudson River; and the plan was to seize him, gag him, and take him in a boat across to New Jersey. Before it could be done, Arnold changed his quarters. He was afterwards sent to lay waste portions of Virginia, and there La Fayette tried to capture him, but without success.

QUESTIONS.—1. Give an account of Marion's escape from some British dragoons.—2. Tell the story about Horry and Baxter.—3. What was at last done by Congress? Where did Gates march? What did the patriots do as he approached?—4. How was the powder used at Hanging Rock saved?—5. What was the date of the battle of Camden? What strange coincidence is mentioned? Give an account of the battle. What followed? Who superseded General Gates?—6. What prevented Congress from sending another army into the field? What difficulties did Congress labor under?—7. What was the condition of Washington's army in the north? What treacherous blow was now aimed at the patriot cause? What post did Arnold command? What offer did he make to the British?—8. Who was sent to confer with Arnold? What took place while Andre was returning? What was the fate of Andre?—9. What did Arnold do, on hearing of Andre's capture? How did Arnold afterwards distinguish himself? How was he looked upon?—10. What plan was formed for capturing Arnold? How was it defeated? Who subsequently tried to take him?

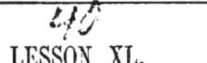

LESSON XL.

KING'S MOUNTAIN.—COWPENS.—GUILFORD COURT HOUSE.

1. After his victory at Camden, Cornwallis proceeded to reduce North Carolina. He sent a detachment to the mountains, to enroll the tories and frighten the whigs. But the whig mountaineers were not easily frightened. They made powder for themselves out of the nitre they found in the caverns, and charcoal burned on their own hearths. Giving chase to the British detachment mentioned above, they overtook it at King's Mountain, and made the whole party prisoners with but little loss.

2. Greene, on assuming command of the southern army, stationed detachments at several important points. One of these, under General Morgan, was attacked at Cowpens by Tarle'-ton, a British officer, famous for his courage and cruelty. Tarleton's men charged with their usual fierceness, but were received by Morgan's riflemen so firmly that they wavered. At this crisis, a charge from Colonel

Washington's cavalry decided the day. The British were defeated, with the loss of many men, and much of their baggage.

3. As Colonel Washington was charging at full speed in this battle, he encountered Tarleton. Both were good swordsmen, but Tarleton was wounded, and had to turn and flee. Soon after this, in a gay company, Tarleton sneered at the American officers, and said above all he should like to see that famous hero, Colonel Washington. "You might have done so, colonel," answered a whig lady who was present, " if you had only looked behind you at the battle of Cowpens."

4. Colonel Washington was as good at stratagem as he was brave. He once appeared before a British redoubt, which was too strong to be taken without artillery. Having no cannon, he cut a pine log, and mounted it on wheels so as to resemble one. Parading this in front of his force, he summoned the British to surrender. The stratagem succeeded. Frightened by Colonel Washington's pine log, they laid down their arms without delay.

5. Tarleton's defeat at Cowpens made Cornwallis very angry. Setting out at once in pursuit of Morgan, he reached the Catawba River just two hours after the Americans had crossed it. Night was near at hand, and he determined to wait where he was till morning. During the night a rain set in, and swelled the river so that for three days it was impassable. Meanwhile, Greene had hastened to help Morgan conduct the retreat. When near the army, he entered an inn, drenched with rain and almost in despair. His kind hostess, after preparing his dinner, brought him all her money, and told him to devote it to the cause of freedom.

6. Greene continued the retreat as rapidly as possible, and crossed the Yadkin. Before the British arrived, another heavy rain commenced, and the river became impassable. Crossing higher up,

Cornwallis pressed on to intercept the Americans before they reached the Dan. But he did not succeed. The Americans, almost sinking with fatigue, reached the ford first, and got across in safety. Here Cornwallis gave up the pursuit. We can hardly form an idea of the hardships suffered by the Americans in this retreat. Their shoes and clothes were worn out. During the whole time, they had eaten but one meal a day, and had slept in the open air.

7. As soon as his men were rested, Greene again took the field. He followed the enemy into North Carolina, and gave them battle at Guilford Court House. The British had the better in this engagement. But their victory was so dearly bought that Cornwallis thought it prudent to fall back. He soon after took command of the detachment that had been sent out under Arnold to ravage Virginia. This was pleasant work for Arnold, Tarleton, and Cornwallis. They managed to destroy ten million dollars' worth of property in the spring and summer of 1781. After this, Cornwallis collected his forces, and fortified himself at Yorktown, Virginia.

8. Meanwhile, Marion and Lee were busy in Carolina. They took one British post after another. The patriotism of Mrs. Motte, a noble whig lady, is worthy of being remembered. A party of British had seized her house. Marion and Lee were besieging them, when they heard that a large British army was but a few miles off. Rather than have them give up the attack, Mrs. Motte insisted on their setting fire to her fine house, to dislodge the enemy. It was done; and the British had to hang out a white flag as a signal of surrender.

9. Among other important posts, Georgetown fell before Marion and Lee. In the attack on this place, the Americans had driven the enemy from an enclosure, and the latter advanced to recover it. "Rush on!" said the British leader; "they are only worthless

militia, and have no bayonets." Sergeant Ord immediately placed himself in the gate of the enclosure. As the British came up, he struck down one after another with his sword, crying, "Any bayonets here? None at all, to be sure." The British recoiled before his single arm, and gave up the attack.

QUESTIONS.—1. After his victory at Camden, what did Cornwallis proceed to do? What was done by some whig mountaineers? What was the result of the battle of King's Mountain?—2. Whom did General Greene station at Cowpens? By whom was Morgan attacked? Give an account of the battle.—3. Describe the encounter between Colonel Washington and Tarleton. What rebuke did Tarleton soon after receive?—4. Give an account of Colonel Washington's stratagem.—5. What was done by Cornwallis on hearing of Tarleton's defeat at Cowpens? How were the Americans saved at the Catawba? What befell General Greene about this time?—6. How were the Americans saved at the Yadkin? After crossing the Yadkin, what did Cornwallis try to do? Did he succeed? What is said of the hardships of the Americans?—7. Where was the next battle fought? What was its result? What did Cornwallis think it best to do? Where did he afterwards go? How much property was destroyed by the British in Virginia? Where did Cornwallis then collect his forces?—8. What were Marion and Lee now doing? What took place at Mrs. Motte's?—9. Relate an incident connected with the attack on Georgetown.

LESSON XLI.

EUTAW.—YORKTOWN.—CLOSE OF THE REVOLUTION.

1. After the battle of Guilford Court House, Greene marched into South Carolina, against the army which Cornwallis had left there to keep the patriots in check. He met with a reverse at Hobkirk's Hill, but, with the aid of Marion, Lee, Sumter, and Pickens, most of the state was soon recovered from the British. Greene at last gave battle to the main body of the enemy at Eutaw Springs. Both parties fought with desperate courage.

2. During the battle, a party of British retired into a brick

dwelling, and closed the doors so quickly as to shut out one of their own officers. As the Americans came up to the attack, he pompously presented himself to their colonel, enumerating all his titles. "Sir, I am deputy adjutant-general of the British army, secretary of the commander, captain of the 52nd regiment—" "Enough," interrupted the colonel; "you are just the man I was looking for. I'll take good care of you;" and holding his prisoner between himself and the British guns, he screened his person till he had accomplished what he wanted, and retired out of danger.

3. The British gave way before the steady courage of Greene's men. The latter, thinking the battle was over, fell upon the captured stores. Seeing them thus employed, the enemy rallied and renewed the attack. The Americans were taken by surprise, but Greene succeeded in drawing off his men with some loss. The British had suffered so much, that the next day their commander destroyed his stores and returned to Charleston.

4. A French fleet, sent over to aid the Americans, arrived off the coast of Virginia in the summer of 1781. Washington had been threatening the British army in New York. Now, however, he marched rapidly to the south, to join the French in surrounding Cornwallis. General Clinton, who commanded in New York, did not discover this movement till it was too late to prevent it. La Fayette's division was already in Virginia. Towards the close of September, the French and American armies invested Yorktown, and a heavy fire was opened from their batteries.

5. Breaches were soon made in the British works. Cornwallis tried a sally, but was driven back into his fortifications. He then attempted to convey his men by night across the York River, with the intention of forcing his way through the French lines at the opposite point, and hastening to join Clinton at New York. One di-

vision crossed the river in safety; but a furious storm set in, and the rest were unable to join them. Those who had landed, after a severe drenching, were brought back in the morning, and no further efforts to escape were made.

6. Cornwallis's only hope now lay in aid from Clinton. He held out as long as he could; but the allied armies brought their batteries closer and closer, and on the 19th of October he found it necessary to surrender. Over seven thousand British soldiers laid down their arms. Washington generously tried to avoid wounding the feelings of the enemy. Before they appeared on the field, he rode up to his men, as they were drawn up in line, and said: "My boys, let there be no insults over a conquered foe. When they lay down their arms, don't huzzah. Posterity will huzzah for you." That same day, Clinton set out to relieve Cornwallis, with a strong force of ships and men. Learning that he was too late, when off the coast of Virginia, he sailed back to New York.

La Fayette.

7. The news of the surrender of Cornwallis was everywhere hailed with delight. The old state-house bell at Philadelphia rang to announce the joyful tidings. Many were so overcome that they could only weep. The aged door-keeper of Congress died from ex-

cess of joy. Washington did not forget to ascribe his success to a merciful Providence; and the troops united in returning thanks to the God of battles.

8. The surrender of Cornwallis put an end to the Revolutionary War. The King and Parliament found it was useless to try to conquer men who would fight in rags, and on one poor meal a day, rather than lose their freedom. Commissioners from both countries met at Paris. The independence of the United States was acknowledged by Great Britain; and peace was established. The British army received orders to evacuate New York, and this was done on the 25th of November, 1783. "Evacuation day" is still kept in New York.

9. While the American army was lying unemployed, a new danger arose. Both officers and men complained loudly of Congress for not paying them according to agreement. They even went so far as to threaten violence, and offered to make Washington King. Grieved at the display of such a spirit, Washington nobly rejected their offer; he dissuaded them from violence, and urged Congress to make provision for meeting their demands.

10. On the establishment of peace, the army, through Washington's efforts, was quietly disbanded. Many a poor soldier left for home without a penny in his pocket. In December, 1783, Washington took leave of his officers. It was hard for those to part, who had labored and suffered so long together. With a full heart, one after another shook the hand of his revered commander. Then, surrendering his commission to Congress, the great leader of the Revolution retired to private life at Mount Vernon, on the bank of the Potomac.

QUESTIONS.—1. Where did Greene go after the battle of Guilford Court House? Where did he meet with a reverse? What did he soon succeed in doing? Where did he give battle to the main body of the enemy?—2. Relate an anecdote about a British officer at Eutaw.—3. Give an account of the battle of Eutaw. What was done by the British commander the next day?—4. Where did a French fleet appear in the summer of 1781? What was at once done by Washington? Whose division was already in Virginia? When was Yorktown invested?—5. What did Cornwallis first try? What did he then attempt? What success did he meet with?—6. What was now Cornwallis's only hope? When did he find it necessary to surrender? How many laid down their arms? What is related of Washington? What did Clinton do that same day?—7. How was the news of the surrender received? What took place at Philadelphia?—8. What did the King and Parliament now find was useless? Where did commissioners meet? What was the result? What orders did the British army receive?—9. What new danger arose while the American army was lying unemployed? What offer did they make Washington? How did he meet it?—10. When was the army disbanded? What was the condition of many of the soldiers? Give an account of Washington's parting with his officers. After this, what did he do?

LESSON XLII.

FORMATION OF A CONSTITUTION.

1. Shortly after the surrender of Cornwallis, Washington, accompanied by La Fayette and other officers, went to visit his mother. Six years had passed since they had met, and now he came the nation's idol. While a great procession paraded through the place in honor of the illustrious visitors, Mrs. Washington remained quietly at home, preparing her yarn. "I am glad to see you, George," were her first words when Washington entered her house; "you have altered considerably." The next day La Fayette called on her, and spoke in glowing terms of her son's greatness. "I am not surprised," she answered, "for George always was a good boy."

2. The war had ceased. The United States were free. But they were still surrounded with great difficulties. They owed an immense debt to foreign governments, as well as to their own sol-

diers and officers. How was this to be paid? Congress had no money, and no power to raise any from the different states, which considered themselves independent, and looked with jealousy on each other and on the general government. England, too, complained that her merchants could not collect what was owed to them in America. It seemed at one time as if the war would be renewed.

3. The people continued to suffer. All kinds of business were dull. The taxes laid in some of the states, though light in themselves, were looked upon as a burden, because money was so scarce. In Massachusetts, a number of people rose in arms and resisted the government. Shays, who had been a captain in the Revolution, took command of them, and the movement was called Shays' Rebellion. For a time they gave some trouble; but the militia were called out, and Shays and his men found it best to submit. The ringleaders came near being hanged, but were finally let off.

4. It was clear that some stronger government was needed. Accordingly, a meeting of delegates from each state was called, for the purpose of drawing up a constitution. In May, 1787, the convention met at the same old state-house in Philadelphia in which the Declaration of Independence had been signed. It contained the wisest men in the country. Washington was elected its president.

5. Different points were sharply discussed by the members. It was hard to please all. At one time it seemed as if they would be unable to agree on a constitution. At length Benjamin Franklin, now an old man, but as firm a friend of his country as ever, proposed that the clergy of the city should be invited to offer prayer for divine guidance every morning before they began their labors. It was done. Greater harmony then prevailed. One gave up one point, and another another. At last our glorious constitution was completed.

6. The constitution was then submitted to the different states. Some found fault with it; but Alexander Hamilton, of New York, and James Madison, of Virginia, defended it from all attacks. It was soon ratified by most of the states. Within three years all had accepted it. It is still (with certain amendments since made) the law of the land.

7. According to the constitution, all laws for the country at large have to be passed by two houses. They are called the Senate and the House of Representatives. Together they are known as the Congress of the United States. They meet once every year. The senators are elected by the legislatures of the different states; the representatives, by the people. The laws are interpreted by Judges, who form what is called the Supreme Court of the United States. The laws are executed by a President, chosen once in four years by electors who are themselves chosen by the people.

8. The President can *veto* a law passed by Congress. It is then null, unless two-thirds of both houses again vote for it. The President is commander-in-chief of the army and navy. He appoints various officers and makes treaties, subject to the approval of the senate. At the same time with the President, a Vice-president is elected, who, if the President dies or is disabled, takes his place. Each state is independent and supreme in matters that concern itself alone. It is only in affairs connected with the country at large that the general government has power.

9. Under the new constitution, Washington was elected President. All looked to him as the only one that could rescue the country from the dangers that threatened it. Again, at his country's call, he left his quiet home at Mount Vernon. His journey to New York showed how the people loved him. Crowds flocked about him, delighting to do him honor. On the 30th of April,

1789, he took the oath of office and became the first President of the United States.

QUESTIONS.—1. Give an account of Washington's visit to his mother. What passed between her and La Fayette?—2. By what difficulties did Congress find itself surrounded? Of what did England complain?—3. What was the condition of the people? What took place in Massachusetts? What was the issue of Shays' rebellion?—4. What now became evident? How was it proposed to form a constitution? When and where did the convention meet? Who was elected its president?—5. What difficulties arose in the convention? What proposition was made by Benjamin Franklin? What was the effect?—6. What was done with the constitution, when thus drawn up? By whom was it defended? How was it received by the states?—7. According to the constitution, by whom are all laws for the country at large passed? How often does Congress meet? By whom are the senators elected? The representatives? By whom are the laws interpreted? By whom are the laws executed?—8. What *veto* power has the President? What other powers does he possess? Who takes the President's place, if he is disabled? In what matters is each state supreme? In what, the general government?—9. Who was elected the first President? What is said of Washington's journey to New York? When did he take the oath of office?

LESSON XLIII.

WASHINGTON'S TWO TERMS.

1. The first thing to be done was to find some way of paying the public debt. This was a hard task, but it was intrusted to a man of genius, Alexander Hamilton. Hamilton gave all the powers of his great mind to the subject. He devised means for gradually meeting a great part of the debt. By his advice, Congress chartered a United States Bank with a large capital. People once more began to put faith in the government, and business soon became brisk.

2. The next difficulty was with the Indians in the west. Even before the Revolution, some adventurous hunters had pushed out from

Virginia and Carolina beyond the mountains, and made homes for themselves in the wilderness. The famous Daniel Boone, with five companions, had settled in what is now Kentucky. His wife and daughter were the first white women that set foot on the bank of the Kentucky River. Many a stirring adventure had Boone and such as he,—many a hair-breadth escape from the wild beasts, and the wilder Red Men, of the forest!

3. One of these pioneer posts was called Bryan Station. In 1782, a party of Indians tried to surprise its garrison. Lying in ambush near the fort, they waited for the men to come out; but the cunning hunters had seen signs of the foe, and kept within the palisades. Unfortunately their water gave out; and, if they went to the spring,

Bravery of the Women of Bryan Station, Kentucky.

they were sure the Indians would shoot them down and make a rush for the fort. At this crisis, the brave women at the post offered to bring the water. Going carelessly past the thicket in which the savages lay concealed, they filled their pails and returned. Five hundred rifles were aimed at them, but not one was fired. The Indians waited for the men, but in vain; and the fort was saved.

4. As the settlements in the west increased, Congress tried to satisfy the Indians by buying their lands. There were some, however, north of the Ohio River, in what is now the state of Indiana, that would not join in the sale. They threatened war, and Congress had to send an army under General Harmer to subdue them. Harmer laid waste their fields. But, while he was pursuing the Indians who had fled before him, one division of his army was defeated, and the other was led into an ambuscade and cut to pieces.

5. General St. Clair an experienced officer, was then sent against the Indians. Little Turtle was their leading spirit. He was a famous chief, whose nose and ears were bright with silver rings. He cunningly planned a surprise. One morning about daylight, when near the Indian camp, the invading army was suddenly attacked. In spite of St. Clair's efforts and the bravery of his officers, his men were thrown into confusion. Many were killed, and the battle ended in a total rout.

6. A third army was then sent out, and this time Washington intrusted the command to General Wayne. Wayne had distinguished himself in the Revolution. His fierce charges on the enemy had gained for him among the soldiers the nick-name of "mad Anthony". Advancing cautiously into the country of the Indians, Wayne defeated them, and desolated their villages for a distance of fifty miles. They were completely humbled. A treaty was signed, and for years the frontier was secure. Wayne is said to have told the Indians that if they ever broke this treaty he would rise from the grave to fight them.

7. When Washington's four years expired, he was elected for a second term. A party had arisen which opposed the measures of the President, and complained that he had too much power. But the mass of the people still looked to Washington as the father of his country.

8. Early in Washington's second term, he was troubled with what was called the Whiskey Rebellion. A tax had been laid on all whiskey that was distilled. Some people in western Pennsylvania said they would not pay this tax. Assembling under a man who took the name of Tom the Tinker, they drove out the collector and defied the government. It was not till Washington sent a large body of soldiers against them that they returned to reason.

9. There were some troubles also with France and England; but Washington met them all with wisdom. Some wanted him to aid the French people, who had driven out their King. Others said he ought to insist on England's yielding certain points that were in dispute. But Washington prudently avoided war. Meanwhile the country throve. It has gone on increasing in strength. The west has become rapidly settled. New states have from time to time been formed. A list of these, with the date of their admission to the Union, will be given hereafter.

QUESTIONS.—1. What was the first thing to be done in Washington's administration? To whom was the task intrusted? What did Hamilton succeed in doing? What did Congress do by his advice? What was the effect of these measures?—2. What was the next difficulty that arose? Where had adventurous hunters made their way? Who first settled in Kentucky? What is said of Boone's wife and daughter?—3. What took place at Bryan Station in 1782?—4. How did Congress try to satisfy the Indians? What tone was taken by some of the Indians north of the Ohio? What was done by Congress? Give an account of Harmer's expedition.—5. Who was next sent against the Indians? Who was the leading spirit of the Indians? Describe Little Turtle. What plan did he lay? Give an account of St. Clair's defeat.—6. Who was intrusted with the command of the third expedition? What nick-name had General Wayne gained in the Revolution? Give an account of Wayne's movements. What was the result? What is Wayne said to have told the Indians?—7. When Washington's four years expired, who was elected President? What is said of the opposition to the President?—8. By what was Washington troubled, early in his second term? Give an account of the Whiskey Rebellion.—9. What other troubles arose? How did Washington meet them all? What did some want him to do? What did others say? What did Washington prudently do? Meanwhile, what was the state of the country? What have, from time to time, been formed?

LESSON XLIV.

JOHN ADAMS.—THOMAS JEFFERSON.

1. Washington would not serve a third term, and John Adams was elected to succeed him as President. Adams was one of the greatest of our early statesmen. During the Revolution, he went to France as ambassador. The vessel that took him over gave battle to a British man-of-war, Mr. Adams having first promised that he would stay in the cabin during the action. For some time he kept his word, but at last he could stand it no longer. Seizing a musket, he rushed on deck, and the captain soon found him loading and firing with the rest. The captain reminded him of his promise and ordered him below. Mr. Adams refused to go; and the captain had to carry him down by force.

2. A difficulty with the French arose in Adams' term. They had an unpleasant way of seizing American vessels. President Adams determined to put a stop to this, and made ready for war. Several actions took place between French and American vessels in consequence of these outrages. In one of these, a French frigate was taken by the Constellation. Lieutenant Rodgers was sent on board with twelve men to take command of the prize and transfer her crew to the Constellation.

3. Before this could be done, a storm separated the two vessels. Rodgers and his twelve men were now in great danger. There were nearly two hundred French sailors on board of the prize, and they might rise and retake the vessel. To guard against this, Rodgers at once ordered all the prisoners below, and placed guards to shoot down any that should come on deck. After three days of fearful anxiety, during which he did not sleep a wink, he succeeded in getting his prize safe into port.

4. Towards the close of the year 1799, the whole nation was plunged in grief by the news that their beloved Washington was no more. He died of fever, brought on by exposure to a slight rain. As his end approached, he said to his physician, "I am not afraid to die." He felt that he had served his country faithfully, and that country will never forget his services.

5. In 1800, Congress met for the first time at the city of Washington, which has ever since been the capital of the United States. Washington lies on the Potomac River, in a small tract called the District of Columbia. This tract was presented to the general government by Maryland. It was at first a wilderness, through which one might travel for miles without meeting a human being. But it has changed wonderfully since then. Thriving farms and pleasant country-seats now dot its surface. Washington has become a large city, and is adorned with fine public buildings. Among these are the President's residence, which you often hear called " the white house ", and the Capitol, a large building in which Congress meets.

6. After John Adams had served four years (1797–1801), Thomas Jefferson was elected President. It was he that drew up the Declaration of Independence. One of the most important events during his term of office was the purchase of Louisiana from the French. Napoleon, then at the head of affairs in France, at first intended to

plant a large colony there. But, a quarrel breaking out with England, he needed all the men and money he could raise. So he sold Louisiana to the United States for fifteen millions of dollars, part of which was to be paid to those Americans whose property had been seized by French cruisers upon the ocean.

7. In the north of Africa, on the Mediterranean Sea, lie what are called the Barbary States. For a long time they were the home of pirates, who used to scour the sea, capture merchant-vessels, and sell their crews into slavery. For a while the United States paid a yearly tribute to secure its vessels from these outrages. But at last the pirates became so insolent that a fleet was sent out under Commodore Preble to punish them.

8. While reconnoitring the harbor of Trip'-o-li, the Philadelphia, one of the American vessels, struck on a rock. She was immediately taken by the Tripolitans. But Lieutenant De-ca'-tur, one of the bravest officers in the service, resolved they should not long enjoy their triumph. One evening, in a little vessel disguised as a coaster, he boldly sailed up to the Philadelphia, and asked permission to moor his boat beside her. Before the Tripolitans found out what was going on, he and his men were on board. After driving off the pirates, they set the ship on fire and made good their retreat.

9. Soon after this, the Americans attacked the Tripolitan fleet and bombarded the city. The gallant Decatur again fought like a lion. In boarding one of the enemy's boats, he was met by the captain, and a desperate struggle ensued. While they were thus engaged, another Tripolitan rushed up with drawn sword and was about to despatch Decatur, when a gallant sailor saved his life by interposing his person and receiving the blow himself. After being pretty severely handled, the bashaw of Tripoli thought it best to

come to terms. For some years after this, the American flag was treated with respect.

Reuben James saving Decatur's Life.

QUESTIONS.—1. Who succeeded Washington as President? What is said of John Adams? Relate what happened to Mr. Adams when he was going to France as ambassador.—2. What difficulty arose in Adams' term? What occasioned it? What took place in consequence of these outrages? What was the result of one of these actions?—3. Tell the story of Lieutenant Rodgers and his twelve men.—4. Towards the close of 1779, what news plunged the nation in grief? Of what did Washington die? What did he say to his physician?—5. Where did Congress meet in 1800? How is Washington situated? How did the general government obtain the District of Columbia? Describe the District as it was. What changes have taken place in the District and in Washington City?—6. Who succeeded John Adams? What is Jefferson noted for having drawn up? What was one of the most important events during his term? State the circumstances under which Louisiana was bought. How much was given for it?—7. Where do the Barbary States lie? Of whom were they long the home? What led to a war with Tripoli?

—8. What befell the Philadelphia? What gallant exploit was performed by Decatur in connection with this vessel?—9. What did the Americans do soon after this? Tell the story about Decatur. What was the result of the war?

LESSON XLV.

JEFFERSON'S SECOND TERM.—JAMES MADISON.

1. On the 4th of March, 1805, Jefferson entered on his second term. Aaron Burr, who had been Vice-president, was not re-elected. Burr was disappointed, and, journeying through the west, he gave out that he was engaged in some great scheme, and tried to induce the leading men to join him. What his scheme was, never was known. It is thought that he proposed separating the west from the rest of the Union and placing himself at its head.

2. Hearing that he had enlisted several thousand men in his enterprise, the President in 1807 had Burr arrested on a charge of treason. He was committed to jail; and this great man, who had been Vice-president, slept for a time in a blanket on the floor among the common criminals. He was tried and acquitted. But people generally believed him guilty; and, though he was one of the best orators and lawyers in the country, he was shunned by all.

3. West of the Rocky Mountains, on the Pacific, lay a province of Mexico called California. North of this was an extensive tract, now forming the state of Oregon and the territory of Washington. Little or nothing was known of this region; and, during Jefferson's term, a party of soldiers and hunters was sent out to explore it. They were gone two years, and met with many adventures. They travelled six thousand miles, and thoroughly explored the valley of the great Columbia River.

4. Jefferson's second term was distinguished by one of the great-

est inventions ever made,—that of the steamboat. When you see our rivers covered with floating palaces, remember that the first steamboat in the world was made by Robert Fulton, a Pennsylvanian, and plied on the Hudson River in 1807. It made the trip between New York and Albany in thirty-six hours, and was a great improvement on the river sloops, which took a week or more to perform the passage. This little boat of Fulton led the way for the splendid steamers that have since become so common.

5. Great Britain still seemed to feel sore at the loss of her colonies. She was the strongest of all countries on the ocean, and took advantage of her power to stop American vessels and search them. She claimed the right of seizing British seamen, wherever they could be found, and carrying them off to serve on her own ships. And, worst of all, she took the liberty of deciding for herself who were British seamen, and sometimes seized Americans instead.

6. The American vessels were often too weak to resist. This was the case with the Chesapeake. Sailing out of port, unprepared for battle, she was overhauled by a British ship, which fired on her, killed several of her crew, and carried off four men claimed as deserters. This news produced great excitement throughout the country. But the British were not always so fortunate. Several years after this, the Little Belt gave chase to the American ship President. After a time, however, she changed her course, and then it was the President's turn to chase. The Little Belt commenced the action as the American ship approached, but soon gave it up with the loss of thirty men.

7. It was clear that unless such outrages ceased war would follow. In the midst of the excitement, Jefferson's second term expired. He was succeeded by James Madison. Madison served two terms, from 1809 to 1817. They were signalized by two wars:

one with the Indians of the west, and the other with Great Britain.

8. The west was now rapidly filling up with settlers. The Indians, again alarmed and forgetting the lesson Wayne had taught them, were ready once more to dig up the tomahawk against the United States. At their head was Tecumseh, the most formidable Indian warrior that ever fought against our country, crafty, eloquent, and a giant in strength. Tecumseh's brother was a noted prophet, and both had great influence among the frontier tribes. They refused to keep the treaty that had been made with the United States, and planned a general rising against the whites.

9. British agents encouraged Tecumseh and his brother to carry out their scheme. The Indians generally were ready to listen to them. While Tecumseh was away, visiting distant tribes, the prophet's head-quarters were fixed at the mouth of the Tippecanoe River, in what is now the western part of Indiana. Here his followers gathered around him and built a town.

QUESTIONS.—1. When did Jefferson commence his second term? What is said of Aaron Burr? What is Burr's scheme thought to have been?—2. How did the President put a stop to Burr's movements? What change of fortune is alluded to? How did Burr's trial result?—3. What lay west of the Rocky Mountains, on the Pacific? What lay north of California? What measures were taken to explore this region? What is said of the exploring party?—4. By what was Jefferson's second term distinguished? By whom was the first steamboat constructed? Where did it ply? How did its speed compare with that of the river sloops? For what did this little boat of Fulton lead the way?—5. What arrogant claim did Great Britain make and act upon, to the injury of American commerce?—6. Give an account of the outrage committed on the Chesapeake. What took place between the Little Belt and the President?—7. In the midst of the excitement, who became President? How long did Madison serve? By what was his administration signalized?—8. What troubles assumed a threatening aspect in the west? Who was at the head of the Indians? What is said of Tecumseh? Of his brother? What did they do?—9. Where did the prophet fix his head-quarters?

LESSON XLVI.

BATTLE OF TIPPECANOE.—WAR WITH ENGLAND.

President's House, Washington City, District of Columbia.

1. The territory of Indiana was at this time governed by William Henry Harrison, afterwards President of the United States. The crafty Tecumseh thought he would commence the war by striking a blow at Governor Harrison. So, going to the capital of the territory with several hundred warriors, he asked for an interview. On a given signal, his men were to fall upon the whites who were present, and let none escape. Governor Harrison met him as desired, but, suspecting treachery, took such precautions that Tecumseh, bold as he was, durst not give the signal.

BATTLE OF TIPPECANOE.

2. Tecumseh had all the pride of his race. At a meeting between him and Harrison, a chair was placed for him by the interpreter, who said, as he offered it, "Your father [meaning Harrison] requests you to take a chair." "The sun is my father," replied Tecumseh, proudly, "and the earth is my mother; on her bosom will I repose." And, wrapping his blanket round him, he sat down on the ground.

3. Wishing to unite the Red Men in one common cause, Tecumseh visited the Creeks, who lived in Alabama and Georgia. Many of them listened to him and promised their aid. But the United States was on its guard. Before the Creeks could take the field, and while Tecumseh himself was absent, an army under General Harrison approached the Tippecanoe River. They intended destroying the prophet's town, unless a satisfactory treaty was signed.

4. Here Harrison was met by several Indian ambassadors, who said that their nation desired peace, and would sign a treaty on the next day. That very night the war-whoop was suddenly heard, and the army was attacked by savages on every side. Harrison, however, was prepared. He had directed his men to encamp in order of battle, and now he hurried from one point to another, urging them to stand their ground till daylight.

5. The Indians, hidden in the long prairie-grass, poured in a deadly fire with the rifle. They had chewed their bullets, so that they would tear the flesh, and every volley they fired caused the wounded to scream with pain. Very few of Harrison's men had been in battle before; still, throughout that terrible night, they kept their line unbroken. When day dawned, they charged the savages. The latter fought desperately. Their prophet had assured them that they would gain the battle, and they believed him. But prophets sometimes make mistakes, and so they found in this case.

6. A vigorous charge drove the Indians from their cover. They fled in all directions. The prophet's town was destroyed, and the army returned in triumph. General Harrison was as merciful as he was brave. Shortly before the battle, a negro deserter, who had been hired by the Indians to murder the general, was seized while lying hidden near his tent. He was condemned to death, and secured, till the sentence could be carried out, by fastening his feet, like a wedge, between the sides of a log that had been partially split.

7. As he thus lay, he kept his eyes sadly fixed on the general. Harrison's feelings were moved. He could not bear to have the negro executed, and asked his officers to pardon him. They were unwilling to do so. They felt that the wicked man deserved to die. Yet, when their general, who had the greatest cause to condemn him, pleaded in his favor, they could not refuse, and the wretched negro was spared.

8. Hardly were these Indian troubles over when the difficulty with Great Britain became more serious than ever. She refused to give up any of her claims. She would search American vessels whenever she saw fit. This settled the question. Henry Clay, John C. Calhoun, and other great statesmen then in Congress, said that it would be wrong for America to submit any longer. Accordingly war was declared against Great Britain. This is generally called the War of 1812, because it commenced in that year.

QUESTIONS.—1. Who was governor of the territory of Indiana at this time? How did Tecumseh think he would commence the war? How did Harrison defeat his treacherous plan?—2. Relate an anecdote illustrative of the pride of Tecumseh.—3. Whom did Tecumseh try to bring over to his plans? How did he succeed? How was this movement defeated? Where is the Tippecanoe River?—4. Who met Harrison at this point? What did the ambassadors say? What took place that very night?—5. Give an account of the battle of Tippecanoe. What made the Indians fight with such desperate courage?—6, 7. What was the issue of the batle? Tell a story illustrative of

General Harrison's merciful disposition.—8. What followed these Indian troubles? What position was taken by Clay, Calhoun, and others? Accordingly, what was done? What is this war called, and way?

LESSON XLVII.

REVERSES ON LAND: TRIUMPHS ON THE OCEAN.

1. The United States does not keep a great army all the time ready, as European countries do. When, therefore, war was declared, there was much to prepare. Those who had charge of affairs knew but little of war; and hence some mistakes were made at first, and some reverses suffered. The first thing proposed was an invasion of Canada. To carry this out, a few regular soldiers and some volunteers from Ohio were placed under the command of General Hull, the governor of Michigan.

2. Hull led his men across into Canada from Detroit. But he marched so slowly that before he reached the first British fort the Canadian militia were in arms. Tecumseh and his warriors lost no time in joining the enemy and cutting off the supplies of the Americans. A British army was also on the march against them. So, instead of attacking the fort, Hull turned round and marched back as fast as he could. The British followed, crossed the river, and appeared in full force before Detroit.

3. The Americans were well posted and were all ready to receive the British with grape-shot as they approached. What was their indignation, when they saw a white flag displayed above the fort! Hull had become frightened, and raised the flag as a signal of surrender. His men wept as they saw it, but there was no remedy. Not only Detroit, with its garrison, but also the whole of Michigan, was given up to the enemy. Hull was afterwards tried.

He was found guilty of cowardice and sentenced to be shot, but was pardoned by the President.

4. Shortly after this, a body of militia gathered on the frontier of New York. Their design was to cross the Niagara River, which separates New York from Canada, and attack the British at Queenstown. Some boats having been procured, the first division of the army crossed. They gallantly drove the enemy from their batteries and seized the heights. But a fresh British army was approaching, and it was necessary to bring over the rest of the men. To the dismay of their officers and their own disgrace, they refused to move. The sight of their wounded comrades, who had been brought back, had dampened their courage.

5. Thus abandoned by their companions, the Americans who had crossed, after holding out as long as they could, surrendered. Nothing more was attempted at that time on the frontier. Both invasions of Canada had failed. Some glorious victories on the ocean, however, made up for these reverses on land. Little was expected of our infant navy, when matched against Great Britain, the powerful mistress of the sea. But courage and will often make up for want of strength.

6. One of the greatest naval victories of the Americans was gained by Captain Isaac Hull, in the frigate Constitution. After being chased by a British squadron four days, and escaping by his good management, Hull fell in with the Guerriere [*gare-e-are'*]. This vessel was one of the finest in the British navy. She had long been on the look-out for "Yankee craft", and expected to make short work of the Constitution. But Hull's broadsides soon made her lower her flag. She was so much injured that he could not take her into port, and the next day he blew her up.

7. Victories were also gained by the Essex, the President, and

the Argus. The Wasp, Captain Jones, had a sharp conflict with the British brig Frolic. Having brought his vessel so close to the Frolic that in loading his rammers touched her side, Jones ordered his men to board. They found the deck a scene of carnage. Only three officers remained there, and one old sailor, coolly seated at the helm. Before Jones could secure his prize, a British seventy-four came along and captured both vessels.

8. The same brave Decatur who had distinguished himself in the Tripolitan war, now commanded the frigate United States. He succeeded in capturing the British vessel Macedonian. Late in the year, another great victory was won by the Constitution, now commanded by Commodore Bainbridge, over the British frigate Java. The Java had to be blown up, but her wheel was first taken out, to replace that of the Constitution, which was damaged in the action.

9. Long after the war, a British officer visited the Constitution. When asked his opinion of her, he replied that she was a fine vessel in every respect, except that her wheel was clumsy. "Yes," replied the captain, "it is clumsy. It is the old wheel of the Java, which we put in, and have kept ever since as a trophy of the victory."

QUESTIONS.—1. What disadvantage did the United States now labor under? What was the first thing proposed? Who was intrusted with the invasion of Canada?—2. Give an account of Hull's movements. What led him to march back without attacking the fort? What was then done by the British?—3. What took place at Detroit? What did the British gain by this surrender? What afterwards became of Hull?—4. What movement was made shortly after this in New York? What was done by the first division of the army? How was their success turned into defeat?—5. What made up for these reverses?—6. By whom was one of the greatest naval victories of the Americans gained? Give an account of the action between the Constitution and the Guerriere. —7. By what other vessels were victories gained? Give an account of the engagement between the Wasp and the Frolic. What prevented the Wasp from securing her prize?

—8. What vessel did Decatur now command? What vessel did he capture? What other great victory was won? What was done with the Java? What was first taken out of her?—9. Relate an anecdote about this wheel of the Java.

LESSON XLVIII.

THE WAR IN THE NORTH-WEST.

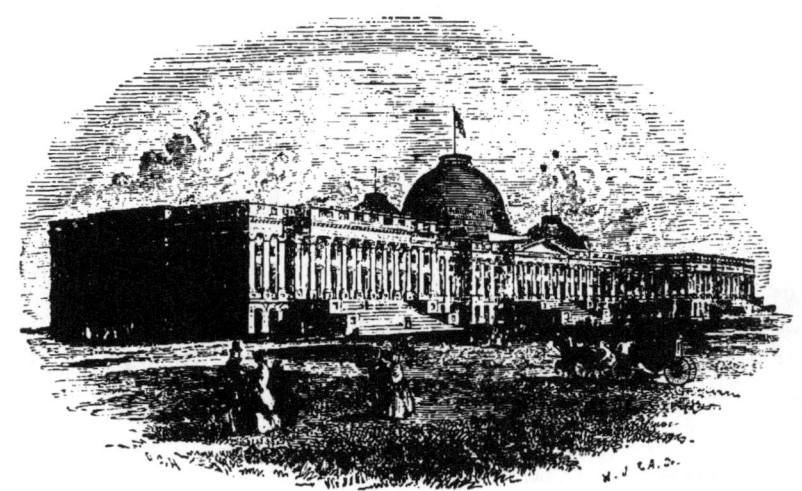

The Capitol, Washington City, District of Columbia.

1. One great cause of the defeats of the Americans in the north-west had been the neglect of Congress to provide a suitable army. It was still backward in acting. There were some who openly opposed the war, and said the President ought not to be supported in it. The frontier, however, now lay open to the British, and it was necessary for something to be done. A body of volunteers from

BATTLE OF FRENCHTOWN.

Kentucky had already taken the field, and General Harrison, the hero of Tippecanoe, was appointed to their command.

2. Harrison's object was to recover Detroit, but his march lay through swamps that seemed almost endless, and when winter set in he was still some distance off. He had, therefore, to wait for spring. The army went into winter-quarters in two divisions, one under Harrison himself, the other under General Winchester. During the winter, Winchester, hearing that Frenchtown, a post to the north, was in danger, advanced to its aid and dispersed a body of the enemy. But he was very soon attacked by a large force of British and Indians under Proctor.

3. During the battle, General Winchester himself was captured by a famous Indian chief called Round Head. Delighted with the uniform of his prisoner, Round Head stripped him of it without delay, and putting it on himself was soon strutting about the field as proudly as a peacock. Proctor, shortly afterwards passing the spot, was surprised to see the American general shivering half naked over a fire, for it was bitterly cold. It was with great difficulty he could make Round Head give up his borrowed plumes.

4. Though their general was a prisoner, part of the Americans still held out. At length a letter was sent them by Winchester, recommending them to lay down their arms. They did so, on receiving a pledge from Proctor that their lives and property should be spared. But no sooner had they surrendered, than Proctor, with his British troops and such of the prisoners as could walk, returned to Canada, leaving the sick and wounded Americans behind, with no one to protect them from his Indian allies. You know the mercy of the savages. Few of the sufferers escaped the flames and the tomahawk. So much was the pledge of Proctor worth.

5. Proctor now thought he was sure of crushing Harrison also.

As soon as the weather allowed, he was on the march for the American camp. But Harrison had not been idle. Weakened as he was by the loss of Winchester's division, he could not hope to take Detroit, but he resolved to hold his ground. Accordingly, he commenced a fort in what is now the north-western part of Ohio, and kept his men at work night and day that it might be ready for the foe. He had no time to spare. Proctor and Tecumseh soon appeared before Fort Meigs [*megz*], as this post was called, and summoned the garrison to surrender. "Not while I have the honor to command," was Harrison's brief answer.

6. The attack was pushed with vigor. The Indians even climbed into trees overhanging the fort, that they might pick off the men. Harrison himself, as he moved around giving his orders, was frequently shot at. Once a ball struck a bench on which he was sitting, and at another time a soldier was killed by his side. He received no harm, however, but baffled every effort of the enemy.

7. News was now received that a body of Kentuckians was near at hand, hastening to relieve the fort. Harrison sent word to them to attack one division of the enemy, while a detachment from the fort fell upon another. The sally from the fort was successful, but those who were advancing for its relief lost more than half their number, the greater part of whom were captured. Proctor allowed the prisoners to be treated so cruelly that even Tecumseh rebuked him. Finding they could make no impression on Fort Meigs, in a few days both British and Indians gave up the siege.

8. During the year 1813, the Americans gained some more brilliant victories on the ocean. Commodore Porter distinguished himself by a successful cruise in the Pacific, in the course of which he took twelve armed whalers. Captain Lawrence, after taking two prizes in the Hornet, was appointed to the command of the Chesa-

peake. In this vessel he met with a sad reverse. The Chesapeake was poorly equipped, and was taken by the British frigate Shannon. Lawrence himself was mortally wounded. "Don't give up the ship," said he to his men as he was carried below. Even at that trying moment his thoughts were on his country.

QUESTIONS.—1. What had been one great cause of the defeats of the Americans? What spirit was still displayed by Congress? What did some maintain? Who had already taken the field? Who was appointed to command them?—2. What was Harrison's object? What prevented him from accomplishing it? How was the army divided for the winter? What was done by General Winchester? By whom was he attacked? —3. What befell Winchester during the battle? Tell the story about Round Head and Winchester.—4. How were the Americans induced to surrender? How was Proctor's pledge kept?—5. What did Proctor now think? What had Harrison been doing? Who soon appeared before Fort Meigs? What was Harrison's answer, when summoned to surrender?—6. Give an account of the attack.—7. What news was now received? What orders were given by Harrison? What was the result of these movements? How were the prisoners treated? How did the attack on Fort Meigs terminate?—8. What success did the Americans meet with on the ocean in 1813? How did Commodore Porter distinguish himself? What success did Captain Lawrence meet with in the Hornet? What befell him in the Chesapeake? What was his last order as he was carried below?

LESSON XLIX.

PIKE'S EXPEDITION.—FORT STEPHENSON.—LAKE ERIE.

1. The invasion of Canada from the New York frontier, in 1812, had failed. But this did not prevent General Pike from attempting it the next year. With a body of men raised for the purpose, he made a descent on the capital of Upper Canada. This lay on the shore of Lake Ontario. It was then called York, but the name has since been changed to Toronto. Landing in the face of a heavy fire, the Americans took the enemies' redoubt, and advanced to

within a short distance of their barracks, which seemed to be abandoned.

2. It was well they stopped where they did, for in a few moments a terrible explosion took place. Logs and stones were hurled high in the air. The British had lighted a slow match before they retired, and thus blown up their own magazine. Several hundred of the Americans were more or less injured. The rest pushed on after the British, and took a number of them prisoners. York, with a large amount of stores, fell into their hands.

3. General Pike was struck down by the explosion. As he lay dying on the field, he heard the victorious shouts of his men. One of his officers asked if he could do anything for him. "Place the enemy's flag under my head," said he. As it was done, his eye lighted up with triumph, and he expired without a groan. After this, the American army took the British posts on the Niagara River. They were abandoned by the enemy, who fell back to the heights west of Lake Ontario.

4. Sackett's Harbor, in the state of New York, was the chief naval station of the Americans on Lake Ontario. This place, left almost undefended, was attacked by a party of the enemy from across the lake. They were driven back by the militia under General Brown. During the attack, one of the British officers, Captain Gray, was shot down by an American boy, who had been a servant in his family in Canada. After the battle, the boy went to his former master, and asked his forgiveness. Captain Gray was dying from the effects of the wound, but gave the boy his watch as a token that he forgave him with his whole heart.

5. After his disappointment at Fort Meigs, Proctor turned his arms against another post at no great distance from it. This was Fort Stephenson, commanded by Major Croghan [*crog'-an*], a youth

of twenty-one. Proctor summoned the garrison to surrender, if they wished to escape being massacred by the Indians when the fort was taken. Croghan replied that the fort would not be taken till all the garrison had fallen, and therefore a massacre could do them no harm. The British at once opened a brisk cannonade.

6. Croghan had but one cannon. To make the enemy believe he had more, he fired it first from one point of the fort and then from another. After a while he saw the British gathering for an attack. Loading his single cannon to the muzzle, he brought it to bear upon them, and quietly awaited their approach. They were soon within thirty feet. At this moment the cannon was fired. Whole ranks were swept down, and a deadly volley from the muskets of the garrison followed. A retreat was ordered, and the next day the siege was abandoned.

7. In the summer of 1813, Commodore Perry was sent to Lake Erie. The British had command of the lake, and Perry was sent to take it from them. The United States had no vessels there. But there were plenty of trees growing on the shore, and out of these Perry built his own vessels. He soon had a little fleet ready, and stood out to give battle to the British. Many Indians were gathered on an island in the lake, to see the engagement.

8. As soon as the British were ready, they sailed out of port to meet the Americans. The action was a hot one. Perry's flag-ship engaged the two largest vessels of the enemy and was badly cut up. Leaping into a boat, Perry then made for another of his vessels. As he passed within pistol-shot of the enemy, he stood proudly erect, heeding not the balls that fell around him. To the wonder of all, he reached the deck of the Niagara uninjured, and the battle was renewed.

9. The breeze now freshened. Perry took advantage of it to

plunge through the enemy's line, and give a raking fire right and left. This decided the day. The British commander hauled down his colors and surrendered his fleet. The number of prisoners taken was greater than that of Perry's men who survived the battle.

10. Perry was a man of few words. He announced his glorious victory to General Harrison in the following brief despatch: "We have met the enemy, and they are ours—two ships, two brigs, one schooner, and a sloop." Men who do much, can afford to say little.

QUESTIONS.—1. Who invaded Canada from the New York frontier in 1813? On what place did he make a descent? Give an account of the first movements of the Americans. —2. What took place when they were within a short distance of the British barracks? Describe the effects of this explosion. What was done by the Americans who were uninjured?—3. What befell General Pike? Give an account of his dying moments. What were next taken by the Americans? Where did the British retire?—4. Give an account of the descent of the British on Sackett's Harbor. What incident is mentioned in connection with this battle?—5. After leaving Fort Meigs, what place did Proctor attack? Who commanded Fort Stephenson? What was Proctor's summons to surrender, and how did Croghan answer it.—6. Give an account of the attack and defence of this post. What was the result?—7. In the summer of 1813, who was sent to Lake Erie? For what purpose? Where did Perry get his vessels? Where were a number of Indians assembled?—8. Give an account of the action. When Perry's flag-ship was disabled, what bold manœuvre did he perform?—9. What movement of Perry's decided the day? What did the British commander do? What is said of the number of prisoners taken?—10. How did Perry announce his victory to General Harrison?

LESSON L.

HARRISON'S INVASION OF CANADA.—CREEK WAR.

1. The British were dismayed at Perry's victory. General Harrison at once followed it up with an invasion of Canada. Proctor and Tecumseh had hastily retreated. Harrison overtook

BATTLE OF THE THAMES.

them at the Thames [*temz*] River. He found the British drawn up on a strip of land between the river and a swamp, held by Tecumseh and his warriors. In extending his line across this strip, Proctor had weakened it too much. Observing this, Harrison directed Colonel Johnson to charge the enemy's front with his Kentucky horsemen.

2. The order was gallantly obeyed. The Kentuckians forced their way completely through the British ranks, and formed in the rear. The enemy, thus finding themselves between two fires, threw down their arms. Proctor escaped only by the swiftness of his horse. The Indians were now to be dislodged from the swamp. Again the fearless Kentuckians advanced to the charge. They were warmly received, and many a saddle was emptied. But, while the battle was at its height, Tecumseh received a bullet in his breast.

3. The chief had expected it. "My body," said he, before the action commenced, "will remain on the field of battle." Stepping forward, he gave his last command, and fell dead at the foot of a tree. His men were seized with horror. The chief who had so often led them to victory was no more. They threw away their arms and fled. The battle of the Thames was won. Michigan was recovered. The western frontier was safe.

4. The Creeks had not forgotten Tecumseh's eloquent harangues. In the summer of 1813, a league was formed against the United States by a number of southern tribes. The settlers in what is now Alabama became alarmed and took refuge in the nearest forts. The crafty Wetherford was at the head of the Creeks. He commenced the war with a cruel blow at the whites. Lurking around Fort Mimms till he found the gates unguarded, he and his Creeks rushed in, set fire to the buildings, and massacred all, men, women, and children, without mercy.

5. A large force was at once called into the field to avenge this massacre. The Tennesseeans reached the ground first. They were commanded by Andrew Jackson, a man of iron will, whom the Indians called "the Sharp Knife". Jackson and his men lost no time in attacking the Creek villages. The Indians fought desperately, trusting to the magic spells of their "medicine-men". But they found that magic availed little against lead and steel. They were defeated in every battle with great loss.

6. Before long, Jackson's men began to suffer from want of food. Their supplies failed to arrive. They could find nothing to eat in the wilderness but acorns. For a time they bore their hardships patiently, but at last they declared they would remain no longer. They had already commenced their march for home, when Jackson appeared before them on horseback. His left arm, which had been

Jackson quelling a Mutiny among his Troops.

shattered by a bullet, was in a sling. His right hand grasped a musket, and he warned them that he would shoot down the first man that advanced another step. The men knew he would keep his word, and, ashamed of their mutiny, one after another, they returned to duty.

7. About this time, another invading army reached what the Creeks called their *beloved ground*. This they regarded as sacred, and their prophet had made them believe that here no foe could harm them. They fought long and well, but were again defeated with heavy loss. In the spring of 1814, Jackson put an end to the war by a decisive victory. A great number of Creeks, with their women and children, had gathered in the bend of a river, and thrown up a breastwork of logs for their defence in front. They were here totally defeated. Their prophet was killed and the power of their nation destroyed.

8. Immediately after this battle, Jackson was sitting alone in his tent at sunset, when a noble-looking Indian entered. "I am Wetherford," said he. "My people are all gone. My warriors can no longer hear my voice. I have come to ask peace for myself and the few that remain. You are a brave man. I rely upon your generosity." Wetherford's request was granted. He was allowed to go back to the forest to collect his scattered countrymen, and through his influence a treaty was made by the surviving Creeks with the United States.

9. In one of the battles with the Creeks, an Indian mother was among the slain. An infant boy was found upon her breast. He was brought to the camp, and Jackson tried to find a nurse for him among the Indian women who had been taken. But they turned away, saying, "His mother is dead; let the child die too." Not so thought the tender-hearted general. Amid all the labors of the

camp, he found time to feed him with his own hands. The orphan grew to be a beautiful and promising youth, and Jackson, who was childless, adopted him. But, before he reached manhood, he fell a victim to consumption.

10. From boyhood Andrew Jackson had displayed a noble spirit. When only thirteen years old, he shouldered a musket in the Revolutionary War. In a skirmish with the British, he was taken prisoner. To break the spirit of the young rebel, the British leader ordered him to clean his boots. Andrew refused, when the cowardly officer drew his sword, and aimed a blow at his head. Andrew saved his life by catching the blow on his left arm; but he received a wound which left a scar that he carried to the grave. You will learn how he afterwards paid back the British for this blow.

QUESTIONS.—1. How did Harrison follow up Perry's victory? What had Proctor and Tecumseh done? Where did Harrison overtake them? How were the British posted? What mistake had Proctor made? How did Harrison avail himself of it?—2. Give an account of the charge of the Kentuckians. What was its effect? Whom did the Kentuckians next charge? How were they received?—3. Give an account of the fall of Tecumseh. What followed?—4. What took place among the Creeks in the summer of 1813? What did the settlers in Alabama do? How did Wetherford commence the war?—5. What measures were taken to avenge this massacre? Who reached the ground first? By whom were the Tennesseeans commanded? What success did they have?—6. From what did Jackson's men begin to suffer? What did this lead them to do? How did Jackson quell the mutiny?—7. Give an account of the defeat of the Creeks on their *beloved ground.* When and how did Jackson put an end to the war?—8. What took place immediately after this battle? What passed between Wetherford and Jackson? What was the result?—9. Relate the incident connected with the Indian baby.—10. Tell the story about Jackson and the British officer.

LESSON LI.

CLOSE OF THE WAR OF 1812.

1. The Americans continued unsuccessful in their attempts upon Canada, till General Brown assumed the command in the summer of 1814. Then their fortune at once changed. Crossing the Niagara River, Brown won the battle of Chippewa; and shortly after again defeated the enemy, who had been reinforced, at Bridgewater, or Lundy's Lane, close to the Falls of Niagara. Late in the year, besieged in Fort Erie by a large force of British, he surprised them with a well-planned sally, drove them from their works with great loss, and compelled them to raise the siege.

2. The battle of Bridgewater was one of the hottest actions in the war. General Scott, now the head of our army, gained great glory in this engagement. Colonel Miller also distinguished himself. He was asked if he could take a British battery which swept the field and threatened the Americans with destruction. "I will try, sir," was his reply. He tried with such good effect that his men were soon firing on the British with their own guns. Three times the British endeavored to retake this battery, and three times they were driven back. Not till midnight did they give it up and leave the Americans in possession of the field.

3. In September, a powerful British army and fleet made their appearance on Lake Champlain, with the view of penetrating through New York to the Hudson River. Plattsburg was the first point threatened. General Macomb [*ma-koom'*] quickly called out the militia, enrolling even boys that were old enough to handle a musket. Commodore McDonough [*mac-don'-o*], by great exertions, got together a few vessels, and met the English commodore,

Downie, who had boasted that with his flag-ship alone he could beat the whole American squadron. But, like most boasters, Downie was disappointed. McDonough gained a glorious victory over him at Plattsburg, and captured his whole fleet. The land forces, which had been repulsed by the militia while the naval battle was going on, retreated in hot haste that same night, leaving great quantities of stores behind.

4. In the summer of 1814, a British fleet appeared on the Atlantic coast, containing General Ross and four thousand veteran troops. Landing not far from the city of Washington, they set out for the capital. A body of militia was hastily raised, and an attempt made to arrest the march of the enemy, but it was unsuccessful. On the evening after the battle, the British entered the capital, the President and many of the inhabitants having fled before them. They set fire to the public buildings, destroyed a large amount of property, and then returned to their ships.

5. Ross then thought he would treat the city of Baltimore in the same way, but there he found the people better prepared. The fort in the harbor successfully resisted the British fleet, and an army of ten thousand men was drawn up to oppose Ross's veterans. While reconnoitring the Americans, Ross himself received a mortal wound. His men tried to force a passage through the American lines, but were so warmly received that they gave up the attempt. The next day, they returned to their boats. Thus Baltimore escaped their ravages.

6. Late in the year, the people of New Orleans were dismayed by the news that an overwhelming force of British troops was about to make a descent on their city. Some thought it was vain to resist, and were for surrendering without a struggle. Fortunately, at this time, General Jackson appeared among them. He at once

assumed the command, erected fortifications, and drilled the militia. He was supported by a number of gallant Tennesseeans, unerring marksmen, who were ever ready to take the field at his call. The British landed about the middle of December, and advanced to within nine miles of New Orleans.

7. After a bold night attack, in which his men behaved well, Jackson intrenched himself below the city, on a ditch which ex-

The Battle of New Orleans.

tended from the Mississippi River to a cypress swamp. The enemy came up and planted their batteries nearer and nearer. But the Americans, though they had only ten cannon, returned their fire with spirit, and inflicted far more injury than they received. On the 8th of January, 1815, the British, led by General Pakenham, advanced to storm Jackson's works. They found the hero ready to receive them.

8. A terrible fire was poured in on the advancing ranks of the British, both from the American cannon and from the rifles of men who seldom missed their aim. The enemy wavered. Fresh troops came up. "See that every shot tells," thundered Jackson. Again the foe fell before those fatal discharges, and they retired in disorder. A few crossed the ditch, but were shot down on the parapet. Pakenham himself fell. The attempt was hopeless, and the British officer who succeeded to the command drew off his men, leaving two thousand on the field. Abandoning the attack, the British made for their ships as quickly as possible. The whole loss of the Americans was only twenty-seven men.

9. Before the battle, Jackson had taken very decided measures with the people. He made some of them soldiers in spite of themselves. A citizen called on him, to complain that his property had been seized by an officer. "Have you a musket?" asked Jackson. "No," answered the man. "Here, guard," cried the general, "get this man a musket and put him in the ranks." He paid no attention to the courts, and after the battle was fined a thousand dollars by one of them for contempt. The amount was quickly raised by the people; but Jackson refused to receive it, and paid the fine himself. Many years afterwards, Congress refunded him the money.

10. The battle of New Orleans closed the war. A treaty of peace had been signed on the 24th of December, 1814. If the news had been received a little sooner, the British might have es-

caped their disastrous defeat. Every one was glad when peace was announced. Bells were rung and flags were hoisted. Commerce had been almost destroyed, and all kinds of business had suffered much during the war.

QUESTIONS.—1. Under whom, and when, did the Americans begin to be successful in Canada? Give an account of General Brown's movements.—2. What is said of the battle of Bridgewater? Who distinguished themselves in this battle? What is related of Colonel Miller?—3. What place was attacked by the British in September, 1814? What measures were taken for the defence of Plattsburg? What boast had been made by Commodore Downie? What was the result of the battle?—4. Where did a British fleet appear in the summer of 1814? Whom did this fleet contain? Give an account of the descent on Washington.—5. What city did Ross next propose to ravage? How was Baltimore defended? What befell General Ross? How did the attack terminate?—6. What unpleasant news did the people of New Orleans receive? What were some for doing? Who appeared among them at this time? What measures were taken by Jackson? By whom was Jackson supported?—7. Where did Jackson intrench himself? What is said of the cannonading? On the 8th of January, 1815, what was done by the British?—8. Describe the attempt of the British to storm Jackson's works. What was the issue of the battle? What was the American loss?—9. Tell how Jackson made one of the citizens a soldier in spite of himself. Tell the story about his being fined.—10. How and when was the war with Great Britain terminated? How was the news received?

LESSON LII.

JAMES MONROE.—JOHN QUINCY ADAMS.

1. On the 4th of March, 1817, James Monroe, of Virginia, became President. During his two terms, the people began to see the importance of canals and railroads. Many internal improvements were commenced. Among these was the great Erie Canal in the state of New York, nearly four hundred miles long. It connects Lake Erie, at Buffalo, with the Hudson River, at Albany. This canal was building during the whole of Monroe's two terms. When

completed, its good effects were felt throughout the north and west.

2. Soon after Monroe became President, a war with the Seminoles broke out. The Seminoles lived in Florida, which still belonged to Spain. Set on by the Spaniards and a couple of Englishmen, they commenced robbing and murdering on the frontier of Georgia and Alabama. Jackson, with a body of Tennesseeans was sent against them, and handled them so roughly that for a while they let the American settlers alone.

3. Not long after this, Spain sold Florida to the United States. The country was now in a thriving condition. Many emigrants came over from Europe. No less than five new states were admitted into the Union while Monroe was President. American commerce, too, was rapidly increasing. It suffered for a time from pirates who infested the shores of Cuba. But, thanks to the energy of Commodore Porter, who was sent against them, these desperadoes were dispersed and their haunts broken up.

4. The summer of 1824 was signalized by the arrival of La Fayette on a visit to the land for which he had bled. Travelling through the country, La Fayette found that forty years had made great changes in every thing but the hearts of the people. They still loved him as their fathers had done. He was everywhere received with honor as the nation's guest. At Bunker Hill he laid the corner-stone of the great monument, and at Mount Vernon wept over the dust of his beloved Washington.

5. Monroe's second term expired on the 4th of March, 1825. John Quincy Adams, a son of John Adams, the second President, was chosen to succeed him. Mr. Adams had been minister to several foreign governments. He served but one term, during which the country continued to flourish.

grounds of the Indians. Long trains of waggons would be seen winding along through the prairies, bearing the sturdy pioneer, his wife, his little ones, and his goods. Sometimes the long prairie grass would be set on fire, and then it was fortunate if the poor emigrants escaped. At other times they found no less fierce a foe in the prowling savage. The Indians would sell their lands to the government and agree to leave them; yet, when it came to the point, they would often fight rather than do so.

3. This was the case with the Sacs and Foxes in north-western Illinois. Under their chief, Black Hawk, they gave great trouble for a time, and kept the frontier in constant alarm. In August, 1832, Black Hawk was taken, and the war ceased, the Indians agreeing to remove farther west. A body of troops sent out under General Scott to take part in this war suffered much from the cholera, which was then raging in the United States.

4. In 1832, Congress increased the duties on imported goods. This produced great excitement among those who opposed the tariff. South Carolina said that the duties should not be collected within her borders. Jackson said he should enforce the law, and took prompt measures for so doing. The difficulty was not settled till Congress passed a bill introduced by Henry Clay, providing for a gradual reduction of the tariff.

5. Jackson was opposed to the United States Bank. He vetoed a bill passed by Congress to recharter it. He also drew out the public money from this bank, thinking it would be safer in the state banks. There was a great storm of excitement when he did this, but Jackson never swerved from what he thought was right. He was equally decided with foreign governments. France, Denmark, Spain, and Portugal, were compelled to pay promptly for injuries done to American commerce. After this the powers of Europe

looked on the United States with much more respect than they had ever done before.

6. The Seminoles had been defeated in 1817, but not put down. When an attempt was made to remove them to lands west of the Mississippi, where they had agreed to go, they again commenced a harassing warfare. United States troops were sent against them; but the crafty savages laid ambuscades for them, and often succeeded in cutting off straggling parties. Then they would flee to inaccessible swamps, from which they would again issue, and commit their ravages.

7. General Scott, always called upon in time of need, was at last sent out to the Seminole country. Though often defeated, the Indians continued the war. In 1838, it was found necessary for an army to penetrate to their haunts in the swamps and forests. This was done, but with terrible suffering to the men. A decisive battle was fought, in which the Seminoles suffered severely. Upon this, they signed a treaty with the United States. Since then, though less troublesome than formerly, they have from time to time ravaged the solitary settlements in their neighborhood.

QUESTIONS.—1. Who succeeded Monroe? How many terms did Jackson serve? Between what years?—2. What is said of the north-west? To what dangers were emigrants exposed? What occasioned difficulties with the Indians?—3. Where did a case of this kind occur? What chief was the leading spirit there? What became of Black Hawk? What was the consequence? What befell a body of troops sent out to take part in this war?—4. Give an account of the tariff difficulties that arose in 1832. How were they settled?—5. What did Jackson do in connection with the United States Bank? What was the consequence? How did he act towards foreign governments? What nations were compelled to make reparation?—6. What difficulties arose with the Seminoles? Describe the warfare carried on by the Indians.—7. Who was sent against the Seminoles? In 1838, what was found necessary? What followed? What were the Seminoles obliged to do? What course have they pursued since that time?

LESSON LIV.

MARTIN VAN BUREN.—HARRISON AND TYLER.

1. On the 4th of March, 1837, General Jackson left the country in the hands of Martin Van Buren, of New York, whom the people had selected to succeed him. Since Jackson, no President has been re-elected. Van Buren and all his successors have served but one term.

2. The chief events of Van Buren's term were a distressing panic and revulsion in the business world in 1837, and a movement on the Canada frontier which threatened to produce trouble with Great Britain. A portion of the Canadians rose against the British government. The people of the United States wanted to help them, and a large body of men took possession of Navy Island in the Niagara River, which belonged to Great Britain. A party of royalists retaliated by crossing from Canada, and setting fire to a steamboat which was used for bringing supplies to Navy Island. War would have followed had not the President promptly prevented the people from interfering in the affairs of Canada.

3. General Harrison, the hero of Tippecanoe and the Thames, was next raised to the presidency, March 4th, 1841. To the great sorrow of the country, General Harrison died just one month after his inauguration, leaving the duties of his office to be performed by the Vice-president, John Tyler, of Virginia. Tyler, like Jackson, was opposed to a United States Bank. When Congress passed a bill providing for such an institution, he vetoed it, and this made him many enemies.

4. During Tyler's term, a troublesome question was settled. This was the fixing of a boundary line between Maine and the

British provinces of New Brunswick. Daniel Webster, one of our greatest statesmen, took the matter in hand for the United States, and settled it to the satisfaction of his country.

5. In 1842, a great exploring expedition, which had been away four years, returned. It had visited various parts of the Pacific before but little known, and made some important discoveries in the far south. Among these was that of a large body of land in the Southern Ocean, extending for a distance of 1700 miles. This is now known as the Antarctic Continent.

6. The magnetic telegraph, that great triumph of the human mind, was first brought into practical operation in the spring of 1844. Its inventor was Samuel F. B. Morse, a native of Massachusetts. To aid him in testing it, Congress had set apart $30,000. A line was established between Washington and Baltimore, and found to work with complete success. Telegraph wires were soon threading the country in all directions.

7. Among the last acts of Congress during Tyler's term was the admission of Texas into the Union. Texas had been a province of Mexico. It was settled chiefly by emigrants from the United States. Oppressed by Mexico, the Texans had declared themselves independent, and maintained their position by several hard-won victories. Still Mexico would not acknowledge their independence. Twice had Texas applied for admission to the Union; and in 1844, the people being in favor of it, she was admitted as a sister state.

QUESTIONS.—1. Who succeeded Jackson? At what date? Who was the last President that served two terms?—2. What were the chief events of Van Buren's term? Give an account of the Canadian difficulty. How was war averted?—3. Who was next raised to the presidency? What melancholy event soon after took place? By whom were the duties of the office then performed? How did Tyler make many enemies?—4. What troublesome question was settled during Tyler's term? By what statesman was this question settled?—5. Give an account of the exploring expedition which returned in

1842.—6. When was the magnetic telegraph first brought into practical operation? Who was its inventor? How had Morse been aided by Congress? Where was the first line established? How did this line work?—7. What was one of the last acts of Congress during Tyler's term? What is said of the previous history of Texas? How often had Texas applied for admission? When was she admitted?

LESSON LV.

JAMES K. POLK.—MEXICAN WAR.

1. James Knox Polk, of Tennessee, became President on the 4th of March, 1845. The admission of Texas into the Union greatly provoked Mexico. A boundary line had never been agreed upon between that country and Texas. The Mexicans utterly refused to treat with the United States on the subject, and threatened war unless the boundary which they claimed was admitted. The United States thought that this was rather high ground to take, and ordered General Zachary Taylor, who had done good service in the Seminole War, to occupy the disputed territory. Taylor promptly obeyed, erecting a fort and establishing about twenty miles from it a depot of provisions.

2. The Mexicans were soon in arms. Taylor's army was small, and fearing that his provision-depot might be taken, he marched with the main body of his troops to supply it with the means of defence. On his way back to the fort, he found a Mexican army twice as large as his own drawn up to dispute his passage. An engagement, the first in the war, at once took place (May 8, 1846). It was followed by a still severer one the next day. In both of these the Americans were completely victorious. They reached the fort none too soon. It had sustained a tremendous cannonading from the enemy, but the garrison had gallantly held out.

3. Taylor soon commenced invading the enemy's country. He had by this time received fresh troops; for, when the news of his first two battles was received, more volunteers than were wanted offered themselves for the war. One place after another was taken, the Mexicans falling back as Taylor advanced, till they reached the strong city of Monterey [*mon-ta-ra'*]. This place was carried by storm, though not without great loss. Taylor continued to advance, and on the 22d of February, 1847, found himself at Buena Vista [*bwa'-nah vees'-tah*] in the presence of the Mexican general, Santa Anna, and an army three times the size of his own. Santa Anna summoned him to surrender. "General Taylor never surrenders," was the reply.

4. Fearful was the struggle at Buena Vista. It was only by steady courage and the skilful handling of their artillery, that the Americans held their ground against the overwhelming numbers of the foe. "Give them a little more grape, Captain Bragg," said Taylor coolly, as he saw a column of the enemy waver before Bragg's well-directed cannon. The setting sun left the Americans in possession of the field. In the morning it was found that Santa Anna and his army had retreated. This was the end of Taylor's campaign, which had been every way glorious.

5. General Taylor was perfectly cool in battle. Once, when the Mexican cannon-balls were coming rather too close to be pleasant, he noticed the officers around him bowing their heads as the balls passed. "No dodging, gentlemen," said the veteran; "a soldier should not dodge." Just then a tremendous ball whizzed by, so close to Taylor's head that before he knew it he was dodging himself. His officers burst into a hearty laugh. The general had to join them. "Well," said he, "you may dodge the balls, if you choose, but do not run."

THE MEXICAN WAR.

6. The chief command in the war was now intrusted to General Scott. He planned an invasion from another quarter, and a descent on Mexico, the capital of the enemy's country. Vera Cruz, on the Gulf of Mexico, defended by one of the strongest fortresses in America, was first invested, and taken after a heavy bombardment.

7. From this point Scott advanced into the interior of the country. He met with no resistance till he reached the Cordilleras [*cor-deel-ya'-ras*], but there had to force his way through a rocky pass at the point of the bayonet. The Mexican army was routed. So hasty was their retreat that Santa Anna left his wooden leg behind. It was found by the Americans and sent home as a trophy.

8. General Scott continued his march till he reached the neighborhood of the city of Mexico. Here the enemy had gathered for a final stand. Their number greatly exceeded that of the Americans, and they were protected by a succession of strong works, which commanded the approaches to the capital. These were taken one after another, by dint of hard fighting and incredible exertions on the part of the Americans. No troops could have behaved better.

9. On the 14th of September, 1847, General Scott and his men entered the city of Mexico in triumph. Meanwhile, the northern part of the country had been invaded and conquered by an American army. The United States was everywhere victorious, and the Mexican government was now willing to come to terms. A treaty was made, by which Mexico gave up to the United States the disputed territory on the frontier of Texas, and the provinces of New Mexico and Upper California, which had been already conquered. The United States was to pay for these extensive tracts between fifteen and twenty millions of dollars.

10. The only other event of importance during President Polk's term, was the settlement of a boundary line in the north-

Entrance of the American Army into the City of Mexico.

west with Great Britain. A large section of country, known as Oregon, lying between the Rocky Mountains and the Pacific Ocean, was claimed by both nations. As it was now rapidly becoming settled, it was important to have the boundary fixed, and this was at length with some difficulty accomplished.

QUESTIONS.—1. Who became President, March 4, 1845? What followed the admission of Texas into the Union? What orders were given to General Taylor? What did Taylor do?—2. Give an account of the first two battles in the war, and the movements that led to them. What had been going on at the fort?—3. What was the next step in Taylor's campaign? What is said of the number of volunteers? Where did Taylor first meet with resistance? How was Monterey taken? Where was the next battle fought? What passed between Santa Anna and Taylor before the battle?—4. What is said of the engagement at Buena Vista? What did General Taylor tell Captain

Bragg? What was found the next morning?—5. What anecdote is related of General Taylor?—6. To whom was the chief command in the war now intrusted? What was planned by General Scott? What place was first taken?—7. What did General Scott then proceed to do? What was he obliged to do, on reaching the Cordilleras? What was the result of this engagement?—8. Where did the enemy gather for a final stand? How were they protected? What is said of the behavior of the troops in taking these defences?—9. What took place, September 14, 1847? What had been going on meanwhile in the northern part of Mexico? What did the Mexican government now do? State the provisions of the treaty.—10. Give an account of the settlement of a boundary line in the north-west with Great Britain.

LESSON LVI.

TAYLOR AND FILLMORE.

1. General Taylor's services in the Mexican War were rewarded with the highest office in the people's gift. He was made President in 1849; and Millard Fillmore, of New York, was at the same time elected Vice-president.

2. California, you remember, was ceded by Mexico to the United States. In 1848, a great discovery was made there. A laborer, examining some sand that caught his eye with its glitter, found it to be mixed with gold. Further search showed that the precious metal was abundant. The news spread. Thousands at once flocked to the land of gold, from all parts of the world. California became rapidly settled, and now, early in Taylor's term, asked to be admitted as a state.

3. The people of the south have negro slavery; not so, those of the north. California wanted to come in as a free state. Years before, an agreement had been made that slavery should be permitted in all territory south of a certain line and excluded from all north of it. Now, as part of California was south of this line, many ob-

jected to receiving it except with slavery as one of its institutions. Angry feelings were roused, which were not allayed till Henry Clay appeared as a peace-maker. Concessions were made by both sides, and a compromise bill was passed by Congress. California was admitted without slavery.

4. While the discussion was going on, the country was called a second time to mourn for its chief magistrate. The good General Taylor died, and Fillmore became President.

5. In 1850, an unlawful expedition was secretly fitted out in the United States, against Cuba. It was thought that the people of that lovely isle were tired of Spanish rule and would gladly seize on any chance of entering the Union. This was found to be a mistake. Six hundred adventurers from the United States landed on the island; but, finding that no welcome except a hot one from the Spanish troops awaited them, they quickly re-embarked. The next year, a similar attempt was made. The adventurers this time were attacked and defeated, and several of them, including their leader, executed.

6. The only remaining events of interest in Fillmore's term were, the fitting out of two expeditions for the Arctic Ocean, to aid in ascertaining the fate of Sir John Franklin, the English explorer; and the death of the three leading statesmen of America,—John C. Calhoun, of South Carolina, Henry Clay, of Kentucky, and Daniel Webster, of Massachusetts.

7. Fillmore was succeeded, on the 4th of March, 1853, by Franklin Pierce, of New Hampshire, who had served as a general in the Mexican War.

QUESTIONS.—1. How were General Taylor's services rewarded? Who was elected Vice-president?—2. What discovery was made in California in 1848? What was the consequence of this discovery? What request was made by the people of California in

Taylor's term?—3. What difficulty arose in relation to the admission of California? How was it settled?—4. What sad event took place while the discussion was going on?—5. What expedition set out from the United States in 1850? With what success did it meet? What took place the next year?—6. What other events of interest took place in Fillmore's term?—7. By whom was Fillmore succeeded?

LESSON LVII.

FRANKLIN PIERCE.—JAMES BUCHANAN.

1. The beginning of Pierce's term was signalized by the opening of the World's Fair. A Crystal Palace, built of iron and glass, was erected for the enterprise in New York. The different states, as well as foreign nations, contributed their products, and thousands visited the exhibition from all parts of the country.

2. One of the greatest events of Pierce's term was the opening of commerce with Japan. Japan is a great empire, consisting of several large islands in the Pacific Ocean. It is occupied by a shrewd but peculiar people, who have always avoided having anything to do with other nations. In the hope of opening a trade with this rich empire, Commodore Perry had been sent out to it with a squadron, bearing various presents and a letter from the President. By skilful management he persuaded the emperor to make a treaty and set apart two ports at which the merchants of the United States might trade.

3. There was great excitement in Pierce's term about the organizing of two territories, Kansas and Nebraska. As they lay north of the old line that had been agreed upon, some said that slavery was excluded from them. But another party claimed that the agreement had already been broken by the admission of California as a free state, and that it should be left to the people of

Kansas and Nebraska to decide for themselves on the subject of slavery. The latter carried the day. But Kansas soon became the scene of a bitter struggle between the pro-slavery and anti-slavery settlers, and much blood was shed before the quarrel was ended.

4. On the 4th of March, 1857, James Buchanan, of Pennsylvania, a distinguished statesman, was inaugurated as President. In the fall of the same year a great revulsion took place in the mercantile world. Banks suspended, factories closed, many merchants failed, and a general panic prevailed. It was some time before business revived and the country recovered.

5. Difficulties with the Mormons obliged Mr. Buchanan to send an army into their territory. The Mormons lived in Utah, far away from the settled portions of the United States. Here they defied the general government, claiming the right of naming their own rulers. When the army, however, arrived in the neighborhood of their chief city, the Mormons changed their tone and agreed to recognize the laws and authority of the United States.

6. Paraguay [*par-a-gwa'*], a South American state, having given our government various causes of offence and refusing to make reparation, a strong naval force was sent out to that country towards the close of 1858. A commissioner accompanied the fleet, to settle the difficulty, if possible, without recourse to violence; and he succeeded in so doing.

7. In the fall of 1859, the United States arsenal at Harper's Ferry, Virginia, was seized by John Brown and twenty-one associates, and an attempt made to excite an insurrection among the slaves. But it totally failed. The movement was put down on the second day, by United States marines. Thirteen of the party were killed in the struggle; Brown and six of his companions were hanged; only two escaped.

8. The summer of 1860 was signalized by the arrival of an embassy from Japan,—consisting of seventy-one persons. They brought the treaty which had been agreed upon, for the President's

Reception of the Japanese Ambassadors in New York.

signature. The Japanese were received as guests of the nation and regarded with universal interest. They were much pleased with their visit, and took back with them many specimens of American art and industry.

9. Another object of interest presented itself about the same time. This was the mammoth steam-ship Great Eastern, the largest vessel in the world. The Great Eastern was built in England, and made its first trip to New York. It was over one-eighth

of a mile long, and attracted thousands of visitors, some of whom came many miles to see this triumph of human skill.

10. When the constitution was adopted, there were only thirteen states. Between that time and 1860, twenty more were added. They were admitted in the following order, and at the date given with each:—

14. Vermont,	. . .	1791.	24. Missouri,	. . .	1821.
15. Kentucky,	. . .	1792.	25. Arkansas,	. . .	1836.
16. Tennessee,	. . .	1796.	26. Michigan,	. . .	1837.
17. Ohio,	. . .	1802.	27. Texas,	. . .	1845.
18. Louisiana,	. . .	1812.	28. Florida,	. . .	1845.
19. Indiana,	. . .	1816.	29. Iowa,	. . .	1846.
20. Mississippi,	. . .	1817.	30. Wisconsin,	. . .	1848.
21. Illinois,	. . .	1818.	31. California,	. . .	1850.
22. Alabama,	. . .	1819.	32. Minnesota,	. . .	1858.
23. Maine,	. . .	1820.	33. Oregon,	. . .	1859.

QUESTIONS.—1. By what event was the beginning of Pierce's term signalized?—2. What was one of the greatest events of Pierce's term? What is said of Japan and its people? What had been done in the hope of opening a trade with Japan? What was the result?—3. What produced great excitement in Pierce's term? What positions were taken by opposite parties? Which prevailed? Of what did Kansas become the scene? —4. Who was inaugurated, March 4, 1857? What took place in the fall of that same year?—5. With whom did difficulties next arise? Where did the Mormons live? What had they done? What steps were taken by the government, and what was the result? —6. To what South American state was a strong naval force sent? Why? How did this trouble terminate?—7. Give an account of the attempt of John Brown and his men. —8. What took place in the summer of 1860? How were the Japanese received? What did they take back with them?—9. What other object of interest presented itself about the same time? Where was the Great Eastern built? How long was it?—10. How many states were added to the Union between the time when the constitution was adopted and the year 1860? Name these twenty states in order.

www.ingramcontent.com/pod-product-compliance
Lightning Source LLC
Chambersburg PA
CBHW031438160426
43195CB00010BB/778